Death and Destiny
in the Bible

Death and Destiny
in the Bible

Michael G. Wensing

A Liturgical Press Book

 THE LITURGICAL PRESS
Collegeville, Minnesota

Cover design by Greg Becker

The acknowledgments for the quotations from Scripture are the following:

Excerpts from the *Revised Standard Version* of the Bible, copyright © 1952 by
the Division of Christian Education of the National Council of the Churches
of Christ in the United States of America, are used by permission. All rights
reserved.

Excerpts from the *New Revised Standard Version* of the Bible, copyright © 1989
by the Division of Christian Education of the National Council of the Churches
of Christ in the United States of America, are used by permission. All rights
reserved.

Excerpt(s) from *The Jerusalem Bible,* copyright © 1966 by Darton, Longman
& Todd, Ltd. and Doubleday & Company, Inc. Used by permission of the
publisher.

Excerpts from *The New American Bible,* copyright © 1970, Confraternity of Christian Doctrine, Washington, D.C.; New Testament scriptural excerpts are from
The New American Bible, copyright © 1970 and 1986, Confraternity of Christian Doctrine, Washington, D.C. Both are used with the permission of the
copyright owner.

1	2	3	4	5	6	7	8	9

Library of Congress Cataloging-in-Publication Data

Wensing, Michael G.
   Death and destiny in the Bible / Michael G. Wensing.
      p.   cm.
   Includes bibliographical references.
   ISBN 0-8146-2093-0
   1. Death—Biblical teaching. 2. Future life—Biblical teaching.
  I. Title.
  BS680.L5W465 1993
  236'.1'0901—dc20   92-27237
                                                        CIP

Contents

Introduction

Hear'st thou, my soul, what serious things
Both the Psalm and Sibyl sings
Of a sure Judge, from whose sharp ray
The world in flames shall fly away!

O that Fire! before whose face
Heaven and earth shall find no place:
O those Eyes! whose angry light
Must be the day of that dread night.

O that Trump! whose blast shall run
An even round with th' circling Sun,
And urge the murmuring graves to bring
Pale humans forth to meet their King.

Horror of Nature, Hell, and Death!
When a deep groan from beneath
Shall cry, "We come, we come!" and all
The caves of night answer one call.

O that book! whose leaves so bright
Will set the world in severe light.
O that Judge! whose hand, whose eye
None can endure, yet none can fly.

Ah then, poor soul! what wilt thou say?
And to what patron choose to pray,
When the stars themselves shall stagger, and
The most firm foot no more then stand?

* * * * * *

O when thy last frown shall proclaim
The flocks of goats to folds of flame,
And all thy lost sheep found shall be,
Let "Come ye blessed" then call me!

When the dread "Ite" shall divide
Those limbs of death from thy left side,
Let those life-speaking lips command
That I inherit thy right hand!

O, hear a suppliant heart all crush'd
And crumbled into contrite dust!
My hope, my fear—my Judge, my Friend!
Take charge of me, and of my end!

(From a seventeenth-century translation of *Dies Irae* by Richard Crashaw)

Death still has its sting. Despite our denials, despite facile assurances at funerals that "so-and-so" is happy now, looking down on us, deep down we know we cannot erase the pangs of death. The Book of Lamentations would resonate more soundly with the human soul in its grief than syrupy poetry about how happy the dead person is: "Bitterly she weeps at night, tears upon her cheeks, With not one to console her of all her dear ones." Thus something like the *Dies Irae* connects more genuinely with human feelings. Musical geniuses like Mozart, Berlioz, and Verdi were moved to great composition by the *Dies Irae,* connecting deeply with the human sympathetic nervous system. For death is the enemy and remains the enemy, as the Christian Scriptures testify (cf. 1 Cor 15:25-26).

The Bible tends to portray death as a reality in a fierce duel with life, even with God. Death is mysterious. The Hebrew, Greek, and Christian portions of the Bible do not make for easy transitions in their understanding of this mystery, especially in relation to an afterlife. The Hebrew portion of the Christian Bible has much to say about human mortality with its strong focus on this life and its faithfulness to the Lord

God. There is not a smooth transition to the resurrection and celebrations of hope in the resurrection, that resurrection which is essential to the Christian portion of the Scriptures. This does not mean that there are not connections or development to be studied. The Old and New Testaments *do* have their meeting places and their development, especially in the Greek portions of the writings which are part of the Christian Scriptures. Some of these portions are larger or smaller depending on texts accepted as canonical in various denominations (i.e., the forty-six books accepted in most Orthodox and in the Catholic traditions for the Old Testament versus the thirty-nine books accepted in most Protestant traditions). This book aims toward explorations of the wider canonical texts (inclusive of the deutero-canonical or apocryphal texts) relating to death and to afterlife out of which various connections can be made.

Above all, the Bible gives us witness that we are not to be without hope. The believer knows through that witness who the victor is in the duel with death—the Lord God. All the powers of death, and of Sheol, are subject to the omnipotent one, who is creator and sustainer of the universe. Life is promised to the faithful, and a day will come when the very power of death will be destroyed: ''He will swallow up death forever'' (Isa 25:7 NRSV).

The Bible takes life and death seriously. The Hebrew portion of the Christian Bible especially accents a decision for life. And life is to be lived in the covenantal relationship with the Lord God for maximum blessing. Yet from the beginning, the Bible does not shy away from the aggressive power of death. However, we cannot presume that our modern questions about death are going to be easily answered in the Scriptures as a whole.

The following chapters show a rich reflection in the texts regarding life, death, and the afterlife. There is, especially, a development in the reflection upon death. Such a development in the text may parallel our own development of questions and understandings. When death occurs in our presence, whether that of a pet, an acquaintance, a close family member, or when we personally have a brush with death, we are immersed in an experience of death which gives rise to questions we may not yet have asked. We reflect, and either we ask further questions or we make judgments based on certain insights from our reflections in order to answer certain parts of those questions. The intensity of our curiosity varies with time, awareness, and confrontive experiences. Such is the case in the historical development of revelation within the Bible.

Just as our own curiosity and reflection about death arises from experience, so did the curiosity of those ancient bearers of the scriptural traditions. Not every question we would ever have was asked immediately by the ancients. However, in time, may of our questions were asked and even some we have not yet asked. In our reading of the text, we can observe then that certain insights were gained and portions of answers were given in the living faith of a people. Other questions and expanded answers developed later.

This books begins a summary of those questions and understandings as they are found in the Bible. It traces the ongoing development of an answer in the text to the eternal human concern about life, death, and our final destiny. It shows that there has been a tremendous development of thought and insight throughout the history of the writings in the Bible, from the early Old Testament to the late New Testament.

Chapter One
Life and Death Perspectives

In Ancient Israel

"If he (God) should take back his spirit to himself, and gather to himself his breath, all flesh would perish together, and all mortals would return to dust" (Job 34:14-15 NRSV) said Elihu, representing as he did the common tradition of understanding among the ancient Israelites about the life and death of each person. Life was a gift God gave and literally breathed into each person. And death was that breath expired by each person in natural death, construed as God taking back that life breath. So we see this common conception in the Hebrew Scriptures situated right in the creation story, in the giving of the original breath, the gift of life:

> Then the Lord God formed man (*adam*—the human creature) from the dust of the ground (*ha'adamah* in Hebrew) and blew into his nostrils the breath of life, and the man (*adam*—the human creature) became a living being (Gen 2:7 NRSV).

In the beginning, in the revelation about life and death in the Bible, there was the sense that human life was a gift and that it was confined to the space of time from conception or birth until death. Life was something sensed as limited to a very determined amount of time. The earliest Hebrews did not theorize about what happens when a person dies. For centuries, in fact, they held to a traditional wariness of afterlife theories. They were people caught up with survival in each given day. They were also a practical, pragmatic people who took life as they saw it. For them, the life-giving aspect of a person was breath.[1] Creation could be understood as God taking dust and shaping it and breathing life into it. At death, a person literally expired—breathed out—that living breath, which returned to God. This was the practical end of the individual's life. However, in revelation, there is not any clear statement about expiration of this breath being the absolute end. In fact, there was an early conception that there was some vague, weak, and shadowy existence in Sheol, which was a kind of underworld.

There is a second consideration which helps to explain the lack of an early perception about a significant life after death. The ancient Hebrew people's view of the human being was that a person was a concrete being, an animated body, an organic unity of body and soul. Often, a modern person might take for granted a later Hellenized understanding of the separation of soul and body which came into the development of thought in late Old Testament times, a separate identity of the soul and the body. This concept owes much to the teaching of certain Greek philosophies (especially that of Plato) whereby there came the idea of death as a release of the soul from the prison of the body, an experience of release that could be anticipated with joy since it spelled freedom for a spirit trapped like a shadow in the prison of the body.

In the early Hebrew concept of the organic unity of the soul and body, there was the understanding that when a person died, the force of life was at low ebb. The person did not cease to exist entirely, but continued a shadowy existence in the place of the dead, in Sheol. This existence was not merely that of a disembodied soul. It was a continuation of the whole body-soul unity. Identifying physical characteristics as well as unique personal belongings were thought to

---

[1]The "breath" of God as used in Genesis and other places of the Old Testament often and rightly is translated as the "spirit" of God, as a kind of animating spirit. The Hebrew word for breath or spirit of God is *ruah*.

survive with the individual. For example, when a prophet was seen in Sheol, he could be recognized by his prophetic mantle (so was Samuel recognized by Saul in 1 Sam 28:14). A ruler would still have a throne and royal robes (e.g., Isa 14:4-21, one of the finest taunt-songs in the Bible). Someone who had died violently would still carry the marks of violence in Sheol.

One scholar on Ancient Israel commented about this ancient thought:

> The distinction between soul and body is something foreign to the Hebrew mentality, and death, therefore, is not regarded as the separation of these two elements. A live man is a living "soul" (in Hebrew: *nephesh*), and a dead man is a dead "soul" (a dead *nephesh*, cf. Num 6:6; Lev 21:11). Death is not annihilation. So long as the body exists and the bones at least remain, the soul exists, like a shade, in a condition of extreme weakness, in the subterranean abode of Sheol (cf. Job 26:5-6; Isa 14:9-10; Ezek 32:17-32).[2]

---

[2]Roland De Vaux, *Ancient Israel: Its Life and Institutions,* trans. by J. McHugh (London: Darton, Longman & Todd, 1984) 56. Further, citing evidence against any belief in the annihilation of the person at death, De Vaux notes, "These ideas account for the care bestowed on the corpse and the importance of honorable burial, for the soul continued to feel what was done to the body. Hence to be left unburied, a prey to the birds and the wild beasts, was the worst of all curses" (cf. 1 Kgs 14:11; Jer 16:4, 22:19; Ezek 29:5). "Yet the corpse which was doomed to corruption, and the tomb which contained it, were both considered unclean, and conveyed uncleanness to those who touched them" (cf. Lev 21:1-4, 22:4; Num 19:11-16; Hag 2:13; Ezek 43:7).

However, as Carroll Stuhlmueller writes (*Bible Today,* May 1991, 150), "Popular piety found ways of getting around these prescriptions. People told stories about saintly persons, such as Enoch or Elijah, who were taken up from earth to be bodily alive with God (Gen 5:24; 2 Kgs 2:11). The bones of another prophet, Elisha, could not be unclean if the corpse of a man, hurriedly lowered into the same grave, "came back to life and rose to his feet" upon "contact with the bones of Elisha" (2 Kgs 13:21). Much earlier, the corpse of Jacob was embalmed and borne in solemn procession from Egypt to the Promised Land, buried alongside Abraham and Sarah (Gen 50:1-13)."

Confirming Roland De Vaux's analysis for honorable burial is Qoheleth 6:3: "Should a man have a hundred children and live many years, no matter to what great age, still if he has not the full benefit of his goods, or if he is deprived of burial, of this man I proclaim that the child born dead is more fortunate than he."

In Israel and the Ancient Near East (ANE)

When comparing the remarks made thus far about the early Hebrew understanding of human origins, life, and death, with the beliefs of neighboring countries of the ancient Near East and their myths on these essential concerns, the revelation we have in the Christian Old Testament is quite advanced and straight-forward. Israel was a people in the midst of other peoples, and there are a number of parallels or accepted notions among the various neighbors of Israel. However, the time period involved makes the comparison difficult, for the stories possessed by Israel's neighbors developed over a period of three millennia (3500–500 B.C.E.). Though the Hebrew people may have shared orally for over a thousand years their understanding of the origin, life, and death of the human person, much of what we have in extant sacred texts became written revelation for them in final canonical form some time after 500 B.C.E.

The person in these more ancient times saw his or her identity not so much in their origins, but in being a part of a community. Their lives were tied up in the community, and the community was the seat of each person's identity and being. Because life was often short and very difficult, the principal preoccupation was with survival rather than speculative realities beyond the pall, and people looked for things to guarantee life for longer survival. Yet the question of life and death was tied up with the question of origins because both ends of the spectrum were seen as part of the one divine order of things. The ancients showed creativity and originality in answering these ultimate concerns.

In all the ancient traditions of the Near East, in the texts and testimonies, there is agreement that human origin came from divinity, whether by divine intervention, creation, or as offspring. In the third millennia (3000–2000 B.C.E.), Sumerian texts show two traditions about origins. In one, the human sprouted from the earth like a plant. The earth's soil was fecundated by the divinity who cried and watered the earth. The divinity plowed the earth and allowed the first human to come forth. In another tradition, the human is formed from clay by the gods. The gods first made a model and then infused wisdom, making a living creature.

The Accadians and Assyro-Babylonians followed the tradition of formation of the human by the gods. There were two currents of understanding. In one, there was the formation from clay alone. In another, there was the mixing of dust or clay with divine blood which came from a rebel god killed for this purpose.[3]

In the Babylonian creation stories, humans were created in order to maintain the physical world and thus relieve the gods of work. In one example, the Atrahasis Epic, the warrior-god Enlil, having the earth to govern as his portion, puts to work a group of lesser gods on an irrigation project. After laboring long on the future riverbeds of the Tigris and Euphrates, they grumble against the management-class gods dwelling in the sky. They burn their tools in protest and demand relief. Enlil caucuses with the other gods and enacts their suggestion that a human labor force be created so that the gods may be relieved. Nintur, the birth-goddess, then mixes clay with the body of a slain minor deity and thus fashions humans.

In another epic (Enuma Elish), the creator-god Marduk eases the task of lesser gods to build a resident city by creating humans. A minor deity is slain, and from his blood humankind is formed. In this epic as in the others, there is the understanding that humans are mere mortals. Their purpose is quite this-worldly, and it seems they are cursed to toil to relieve the arbitrary gods of some of their original labors. One might find both a parallel and contrast in the second Genesis creation-account (Adam's creation) where he is placed in God's garden to till and keep it (Gen 2:15). The great difference here is that one could presume toil is a good. This was

[3]Pritchard, ed. *ANET* (Ancient Near Eastern Texts), 2nd. ed., 104–06, plus suppl. volume, pp. 512–14.

seen as natural, part of the gift, and not yet a curse. The curse
came later after the sin of the humans in the garden. And
here the curse is not the toil as such but betrayal of toil, the
rebellion of the soil, or the cursed mixed results of labor and
productivity.

Very little is known of ancient Egyptian myths of human
origins. There seems to have been a tradition that humans
originated from the tears of the great creator god or that humans came forth from the bodily members of the supreme god.

For the Hebrew people, the human being came as a result
of divine creation by the Lord God. The story of origins is
told in their Scriptures. In the earlier account of the creation
of the human in Genesis (2:4b-25), the Lord God uses the
element of clay (or dust, the *ha'adamah* in Hebrew) for material but God's own breath or spirit for life and animation.
The human became a living being (the Hebrew is *nephesh*,
cf. Gen 2:7). The true life power is the wind, spirit, or breath
of the Lord God, which was in the beginning blowing over
the face of the earth:

> In the beginning God created the heavens and the earth; the earth was
> a formless void and darkness covered the face of the deep, while a
> wind from God swept over the face of the waters (Gen 1:1-2 NRSV).[4]

The idea of divine blood as part of the creating material for
the human was not central to early Hebraic thought, although
blood was recognized later as the seat of life and thus belonged
to God.[5]

---

[4]In the Psalms there is rich imagery acknowledging this creative spirit, breath of
God. "When you send forth your spirit, they are created, and you renew the face
of the earth" (Ps 104 NAB). Job appeals to God's memory of creating and form-
ing humanity from clay: "Your hands have formed me and fashioned me. . . .
Oh, remember that you fashioned me from clay!" (Job 10:8-9 NAB).

[5]Blood was poured on the ground when slaughtering animals as a sign of returning "life" to God. Likewise, the blood would be splashed on the base of the altar
in sacrificial offerings and occasionally the people were sprinkled with it—all relating the blessings of life given by and returned to the Lord God. In eating a sacred
meal the blood was not ever to be consumed because the Mosaic law so prescribed:
"But make sure that you do not partake of the blood; for blood is life, and you
shall not consume this seat of life with the flesh" (Deut 12:23 NAB).

Chapter Two
The Ancient Hebrew Focus on Life

The primary focus of the consciousness of the ancients among the Hebrews was a focus on this life, not on an afterlife. Thus it would be unfair to look for biblical texts which deal only with the Hebrew concept of death without an examination of texts pertaining to life. Their attitude toward life avoided any sense of morbidity. Likewise, neither was there morbidity when the literature spoke of death. In fact, there was a great affirmation of life. I tend to agree with Walter Brueggemann's assessment that within the biblical historical context and its faith-understanding, death was "not particularly feared."[6] There was a tremendous affirmation of hope in life to be lived. So Qoheleth reflects, "Whoever is joined with all the living has hope, for a living dog is better than a dead lion" (Qoh 9:4 NRSV).

In the heart of the ancient Hebrew, life was a gift of God, to be lived on this earth: "The heavens are the Lord's heavens, but the earth he has given to human beings" (Ps 115:16 NRSV). Life was concrete and pragmatically understood as extending from natural birth to death. And life was tied to external manifestations of bodily life. So if breathing stopped, human life did, too: "When you take away their breath, they die and return to their dust" (Ps 104:29 NRSV) or "If [God] were to take back his spirit to himself, and gather

---

[6]Walter Brueggemann, "Death, Theology of" *Interpreter's Dictionary of the Bible, Supplementary Volume.*

to himself his breath, all flesh would perish together, and all mortals would return to dust" (Job 34:14-15 NRSV).

Life in its fullness and wholeness, therefore, appeared as strength that would decrease with sickness, old age, sleep. The ultimate attainment of a quality life was life with God in the living community of faith, and life's blessing then was longevity:

> Honor your father and your mother, that you may have a long life in the land which the Lord, your God, is giving you (Exod 20:12 NAB).

> He asked life of you: you gave it to him, length of days forever and ever (Ps 21:4 NRSV).

> The Lord is my life and salvation; whom shall I fear. The Lord is the strength of my life (Ps 27 NRSV).

God sets before the human being life or death (cf. Deut 30:15). Death is not opposed to life; rather, it is just at the other end of the continuum of life. Death is the life force struck down to a minimum.

Thus would be the condition of the dead in the place of Sheol—life at its lowest ebb. Therefore one can understand Hezekiah's prayer during and after his sickness:

> I said, "In the noontide of my days I must depart; I am consigned to the gates of Sheol for the rest of my years." I said, "I shall not see the Lord in the land of the living" (Isa 38:10-11 NRSV).

On earth, the human person has a particular alloted time:

> There is an appointed time for everything, and a time for every affair under the heavens. A time to be born, and a time to die; a time to plant, and a time to uproot. . . .

> He has made everything appropriate to its time (Qoh 3:1-2 and 3:11 NAB).

It is a good time if the person is in good relationship with God: "The fear of the Lord prolongs days, but the years of the wicked will be shortened" (Prov 10:27 NAB).

If the human has his time, it was understood that God had his own time as well. There was the time of the creation of the world (cf. Gen 1:1f, 2:4a). God's time is prior and determines all other times:

> The day is yours, the night, too. You have established the light and the sun (Ps 74:16 NAB).
>
> He changes times and seasons (Dan 2:21 NAB).
>
> In a time of favor I have answered you (Isa 49:8 NAB).
>
> I pray to you, O Lord, for the time of your favor (Ps 69:13 NAB).

Finally, the limits of the human person's particular time was set forth by God in Genesis 6:3: "Then the Lord said: 'My spirit shall not abide in mortals forever, for they are flesh; their days shall comprise one hundred and twenty years'" (NRSV).

The fullness of life, though, was living toward this maximum. There is the "blessing" vision of Isaiah when God renews the people and their world:

> No longer will there be . . . an infant who lives but a few days, or an old man who does not round out his full lifetime; He dies a mere youth who reaches but a hundred years, and he who fails of a hundred shall be thought accursed (Isa 65:20 NAB).

The time of life on earth is to be occupied by sensible work. God sent the human out of the garden to work. "The Lord God sent him (*adam*) forth from the garden of Eden, to till the ground from which he (*adam*) was taken" (Gen 3:23 NRSV). Work was considered a good imitation of God who worked in creating the world. The imitation was to also honor the rhythm of God's original work week—six days of labor and one day of Sabbath. Sabbath has the Hebrew meaning of ceasing and desisting whatever we are doing in our labors. It is a day for rest. Sabbath also came to mean a day of reflection, worship, and enjoyment of freedom. Still later in Hebrew thought and revelation, this day and its proper observance was established firmly as one of the pillar signs of the covenant, along with circumcision. In the wisdom tradition of Israel, Qoheleth reflected that despite God's unfathomable ways one should be glad and do well in life's labors:

> I have seen the business that God has given to everyone to be busy with.
>
> I know that there is nothing better for them than to be happy and enjoy themselves as long as they live; moreover, it is God's gift that all should eat and drink and take pleasure in all their toil (Qoh 3:10 and 3:12-13 NRSV).

This same Wisdom writer later re-enforced his advice:

> Enjoy life with the wife whom you love, all the days of your vain life that are given you under the sun, because that is your portion in life and in your toil at which you toil under the sun. Whatever your hand finds to do, do with your might; for there is no work or thought or knowledge or wisdom in Sheol, to which you are going (Qoh 9:9-10 NRSV).

Ancient Israel parted company with the neighboring cultures in having a dynamic, freer, and existential conception of human existence. The human was not the work-slave of the fickle toilmaster gods. The human was given a vocation of co-dominance and co-responsibility with the Lord God in relation to creation and work:

> God blessed them, and God said to them, "Be fruitful and multiply, and fill the earth and subdue it; and have dominion over the fish of the sea and over the birds of the air and over every living thing that moves upon the earth." God said: "See, I have given you every plant yielding seed that is upon the face of all the earth. . . . You shall have them for food" (Gen 1:28-29 NRSV, cf. Gen 1:26).

In this, the great dignity of the human vocation and of the human person was recognized.

In the Psalms, the people celebrated this dignity of the human person created by God:

> What are human beings that you are mindful of them, mortals that you care for them? Yet you have made them a little lower than God, and crowned them with glory and honor. You have given them dominion over the works of your hands, you have put all things under their feet (Ps 8:4-6 NRSV).

To be lazy or slothful was considered a violation of the human vocation of work and thus was seen as a sin: "Go to the ant, you lazybones; consider its ways and be wise" (Prov 6:6, cf. Prov 10:4, 12:24, 20:4; Qoh 10:18, 11:4).

Because the Lord God is not fickle, there can be a trust in the rhythm and gift of life. We see this trust in a number of verses in the sacred revelation to the ancient Israelites:

> As long as the earth lasts, seedtime and harvest, cold and heat, summer and winter, and day and night shall not cease (Gen 8:22 NAB).

> When I lie down in sleep, I awake again, for the Lord sustains me (Ps 3 NAB).

> As soon as I lie down, I fall peacefully asleep, for you alone, O Lord, bring security to my dwelling (Ps 4:9 NAB).

> When you lie down, you need not be afraid, when you rest, your sleep will be sweet (Prov 3:24 NAB).

> Whoever obeys me dwells in security, in peace, without fear of harm (Prov 1:33 NAB).

The ancient Israelite wished to drink deeply of life and its joys. They had a basic optimism (cf. Isa 65:17, "Behold, I am about to create new heavens and a new earth"). Yet there was a realism, too, about the sorrows of life. Sometimes sorrows became almost overwhelming. Elijah begged that God take his life when he became overwhelmed by his troubles (cf. 1 Kgs 19:4). Jeremiah, too, felt sad he had ever been born (cf. Jer 15). Psalm prayers lament life, its sorrows, and the seeming abandonment by God (cf. Pss 3, 22). And the Wisdom writer Qoheleth observed, "Again I considered all the oppressions that take place under the sun: the tears of the victims with none to comfort them!'' (Qoh 4:1 NAB) Many felt Job's discouragement and his sigh, ''A mortal, born of woman, few of days and full of trouble, comes like a flower and withers'' (Job 14:1-2 NRSV).

Through all this, the basic theological understanding in ancient Israel was that life was a gift, that the human person was weak and vulnerable and must accept the limits of life. Life was to be accepted with its joys and its sorrows. Life attained its true sense when it was accepted and embraced. As life was to be accepted, so was death to be accepted. God's mystery in all of this is also to be accepted, for God's ways are so far above human intelligence as to be incomprehensible. Job's elegant prayer summarizes this acceptance: ''Naked I came from my mother's womb, and naked shall I return there; the Lord gave, and the Lord has taken away; blessed be the name of the Lord!'' (Job 1:21 NRSV).

Chapter Three
Human Destiny in the Old Testament

Ancient neighbors of Israel and even those pre-dating Israel's existence as a nation believed (a belief seemingly present among all primitive peoples) in some form of *post mortem* survival. However, most of these peoples believed that any meaningful existence was this-worldly. Such was the case in the civilization and stock of the Assyro-Babylonians from which Abraham and the patriarchs apparently came and with which they seemed to maintain some association.

Since the Assyro-Babylonian[7] believed that humans were fashioned to do labor for the gods (till the land, construct temples, etc.) it seems they perceived all meaningful existence to be in this world. They sensed that their life would have meaning for the gods only so long as they were useful. It was hard to conceive that the gods would provide any kind of meaningful existence either as a reward or punishment after death. In the ancient writings there is, therefore, a sustained revolt against death. However, they, like the Sumerians before them, did not view their death as complete annihilation. With death and the dissolution of the body, the person became a fearsome ghostly image (*etemmu*). Usually such a ghostly image stayed in the area of the corpse burial and had

---

[7]Cf. James Pritchard, ed. *Ancient Near Eastern Texts,* 2nd ed. for such epics as the Gilgamesh Epic, Atrahasis Epic, and Enuma Elish.

a connection to and presence in the underworld.[8] There was also a perception that this kind of ghostly remains could leave the burial area and terrorize the living.

The vast "below" or underworld was understood as a extensive city beneath the earth. Sometimes it was called "The Great Below" and contrasted to "The Great Above." Entrance might be through the burial tomb, cave, or a crevice in the earth. The realm was thought to be surrounded by seven walls, each with a gate through which the deceased might enter and where they were divested of their clothes by a demon-gatekeeper. Such was their conception of one's vulnerability after death. This in some way also symbolized the equality of the deceased as they entered the place of no return. Into this dark and dusty place which was filled with terror, they were ushered into the presence of the presiding deities.[9] There may have been a common conception that some sort of judgment took place, though we do not know what it was based upon. It did not really relate to any moral conduct in the land of the living as later Jewish and Christian people would believe about afterlife judgment.

The ancient Canaanites, too, had a similar conception of the underworld as a rather unpleasant place. In addition, they had a widespread fear of demons, typical of the neighbors of ancient Israel. Such bodiless demons were held responsible for many of the evil thoughts or actions of human beings. The Canaanite attributed death to *Mot,* god of death and drought, who looked for the opportunity to crush victims. Besides *Mot,* there were other gods of the underworld and of warfare and pestilence (e.g., Rephesh, god of the plague) which always posed danger to the living.

---

[8] R. H. Charles, *Eschatology* (New York: Schocken Books, 1963) 31–32. Herein there is developed the idea from ancient thought that the underworld is an interrelation of all tombs. Maybe the underworld ideas came from observation of cave or rock-hewn tomb burials. Thus the "below" was perceived as dark, slimy, and silent.

[9] Mythologies as found in *Ancient Near Eastern Texts,* James Pritchard, ed.; 2nd ed.

Among the Greeks of the Homeric age there were the shadowy images of the dead, often referred to as the "shades," as well as descriptive portrayals of the underworld.[10]

Among all these various neighbors of Israel in ancient times, there can be perceived a kind of depression about the future destiny of the human mortal, and a basic death anxiety, given the conception of such a dreary, if not terror-filled, afterlife. Though the ancient Israelites shared some aspects of these afterlife understandings with their neighbors, one can read of their unique and different understanding, de-mythologizing much of what their ancient neighbors conceived about the afterlife. The basis of this difference would seem to be their unique belief in the one, true, and faithful God, sometimes called the religion of Yahwism (cf. Exod 3:14: "I am who am"—the basis for the name of God as Yahweh).

The canonical literature (referring to the books held by Christians as the sacred texts) of the Old Testament contains more than one perspective on death because the material comes from a long period of history—at least a thousand years of development. Also, the development is not an even or smooth one. Various views were held in later Old Testament thought and on into New Testament times by different groups. For example, the Sadducees (a Jewish sect) held to an ancient stance in the Old Testament that the underworld (Sheol) is the final abode of all the dead (who are at most semi-conscious), long after the Pharisees (followed by Christianity) accepted the innovative position that there would be a resurrection of the dead. Yet, in the early part of this summary, we presented the first understanding of the Ancient Hebrews. Later, we will summarize the more-developed view of the Old and New Testaments.

In all ages of the biblical texts, there is recognition that death is an everyday reality and that God knows the days of the life of each human and even sets the boundaries of the life

[10]*The Odyssey*, trans. Samuel Butler, rev. Malcolm Willcock (New York: Washington Square Press, 1964).

span: "Since their days are determined, and the number of their months is known to you, and you have appointed the bounds that they cannot pass" (Job 14:5 NRSV). The reality of death was never made mythical in the thought of early written revelation as it was among Israel's neighbors. Nor was it presented as something desirable except in some cases where it was seen as a release from suffering. We have seen this in Elijah who begged that he might die for he had had enough of life (cf. 1 Kgs 19:4). And there are other instances such as in Jonah (4:3, 8), Job (7:15), Qoheleth (3:19-21), and Isaiah (38:10). In general, in Old Testament thought, death was thought of as normal and something to be accepted, especially if one could live out the fullness of his or her days. It was thought of as a horror or disgrace if death was premature or tragic or occurred away from one's homeland and people or when one had no heirs. This reality of death (i.e., mortality), and the necessary acceptance of it, is reflected in the Genesis dictum, "You are dust and to dust you will return" (Gen 3:19 NRSV; cf. Qoh 3:20).

Death, in the Old Testament, could be accepted with a certain tranquility if it was a normal death. Thus spoke Joshua at the end of his days:

> And now I am about to go the way of all the earth, and you know in your hearts and souls, all of you, that not one thing has failed of all the good things which the Lord your God promised concerning you. . . . (Josh 23:14 NAB)

God foretold of Abram, "As for yourself, you shall go to your fathers in peace; you shall be buried in a good old age" (Gen 15:15). And so it came to be in Genesis 25:8 (NAB): "Abraham breathed his last and died in a good old age, an old man and full of years, and was gathered to his people." The book of Job speaks this wisdom: "You shall approach the grave in full vigor, as a shock of grain comes in at its season" (Job 5:26 NAB). The suffering servant of Isaiah is promised such a blessing: "He shall see the light in fullness of days" (53:11 NAB). The Book of Sirach advises the wisdom of accepting death in its time: "Fear not death's decree for you; remember, it embraces those before you, and those after" (41:3 NAB).

Part of the reason that the ancients among the Israelites found it difficult to grasp a separate existence apart from the body and its life is based on a kind of monistic thinking common at that time. That is, as we noted in the first chapter, life was what was observed around them. The person was a whole unit, a body-soul complex. The body and soul were one reality. The idea of two realities here, understood as possible separate realities of the person, came very late in Old Testament thought. Therefore, in the context of this more-ancient understanding, the woman of Tekoa could share with King David a common cliche which presented an ancient view of the finality of death:

> We must indeed die; we are then like water that is poured out on the ground and cannot be gathered up. Yet, though God does not bring back life he does take thought how not to banish anyone from him (2 Sam 14:14 NAB).

It was difficult in these early times to imagine any existence which meant a division of the body-life-soul complex.

With this understanding, we can observe how the early conception of immortality could barely transcend this world. Emphasis was placed on the joy of this life. The Psalmist prays that such a life be given by God: "Fill us at daybreak with your kindness, that we may shout for joy and gladness all our days" (Ps 90:14 NAB). There is the command of God in the Torah of Moses to make a choice for this life and its blessings:

> I have set before you life and death, the blessing and the curse. Choose life, then, that you and your descendants may live, by loving the Lord, your God, heeding his voice, and holding fast to him (Deut 30:15-16 NAB).

The conceptions about an afterlife were vague. The focus tended to be on gaining immortality by being remembered

by one's descendants. This meant that beyond the importance placed on survival and aid in old age, transcendent importance was placed on being blessed with many descendants.
Having a descendant was the primary concern of Abraham
in the Book of Genesis. God often repeated his promise of
descendants throughout the development of the covenant
with Abraham. Finally, God promises descendants and therefore, through Abraham and his descendants, the earth would
find blessing:

> I will bless you abundantly and make your descendants as countless
> as the stars of the sky and the sands of the seashore; your descen-
> dants shall take possession of the gates of your enemies, and in your
> descendants all the nations of the earth shall find blessing—all this
> because you obeyed my command (Gen 22:17-18 NAB).

The suffering servant of Isaiah is rewarded in seeing his days
prolonged in his descendants: "He shall see his descendants
in a long life" (53:10 NAB).

Though the understanding of death as a natural result of
life on earth was normal, that understanding did not mean
all death was accepted as normal. There were two types of
death not accepted in ancient Old Testament times. One happened abnormally, contrary to the hope for a full life with
natural death in old age. This might be a premature death
when a person could not fulfill all the days of a full life before God, or when that life ended tragically or in some hor-
rible manner.

Sometimes this non-normal death was the death of the im-
pious. This last notion was developed more in the sense that
death already existed in the lives of persons living outside of
a relationship with the God of the Covenant. Wickedness
brought about doom in such people's lives. This was a
presumption in one book, The Wisdom of Solomon:[11]

[11]The Book of Wisdom is an apocryphal book of writings for the Hebrew canon
as well as for many Bibles of a number of Christian denominations, yet canonical
for the various Orthodox branches of Christianity and for Roman Catholics, often
called a deuterocanonical book in their traditions.

"Court not death by your erring way of life, nor draw to yourselves destruction by the works of your hands" (1:12 NAB). There was not, however, any full theological development of a relationship between sin and physical misfortune or even death. This was a strong assumption, however, of classical Wisdom literature. This theological development did not continue in the works of Job or Qoheleth, these latter often questioning the assumptions of classical wisdom. In fact, Qoheleth later specifically questioned the automatic presumption of that relationship (cf. Qoh 7:15, 9:2-3).

When God commands, in Genesis 2:17 (NAB), "From that tree you shall not eat; the moment you eat from it you are surely doomed to die," we are able to see an understanding that an abnormal or premature death is a severe warning. King Hezekiah lamented a possible premature death when he prayed, "In the noontime of life I must depart! To the gates of the nether world I shall be consigned for the rest of my years" (Isa 38:10 NAB). And Hagar pleaded to the Lord against the untimely death of her child: "Let me not watch the child die" (Gen 21:16 NAB).

When Jephthah the Gileadite foolishly vowed to offer a human sacrifice to the Lord if he was victorious, promising that the person sacrificed would be the first person to greet him from his house when he returned from battle, it turned out to be his young daughter—rather than a servant—who innocently greeted him. When she learned of the vow, she was willing to sacrifice herself, but asked her father for two months that she might mourn her virginity with her companions. This request she was granted (Judg 11).

Jephthah's daughter was mourning her untimely death when she requested to mourn her virginity for she was mourning the loss of what was understood in those times as the fulfilling purpose of a young woman's life—marriage and children. And such is the lament in Psalm 89 for young life cut short: "You have shortened the days of his youth" (Ps 89:46 NAB).

The second kind of death not acceptable to the ancient Israelite was death without a surviving heir. Such was Abram's anxiety before God: "O Lord God, what will you give me, for I continue childless. . . . You have given me no offspring" (Gen 15:2-3 NRSV). Or such was Absalom's sadness in 2 Samuel 18:18: "During his lifetime Absalom had taken a pillar and erected it for himself in the King's Valley, for he said, 'I have no son to perpetuate my name'" (NAB).

Various Israelite institutions were established to combat such a fate: adoption, polygamy, concubines through whom a barren wife could satisfy a husband's desire for male offspring, and levirate marriage. Thus Abraham in the Book of Genesis had relations with Sarah's maid Hagar whom Sarah gave to her husband. And Boaz was conscious of his levirate obligation when he married Ruth:

> Ruth . . . I have bought to be my wife, to perpetuate the name of the dead in his inheritance, that the name of the dead may not be cut off from among his brethren and from the gate of his native place (Ruth 4:10 NAB).

So far, we have observed how death was seen as the natural destiny of the human being in ancient Israelite thought. The focus was life and life in covenant relationship with one's people and one's God. And as we have noted from Deuteronomy, God commanded the people to choose life and enjoy it to the full by following the commandments given through Moses.

One's purposeful destiny in life was to sing the praises of the God of the Covenant who saves and delivers his people and gives life in response to faithfulness. In life, one could properly praise God. There was clear doubt from earliest times whether the dead could continue to do so as they were perceived as not fully conscious, vital beings:

> It is not the dead who praise the Lord, nor those who go down into silence; but we bless the Lord, both now and forever (Ps 115:17-18 NAB).

Will you work wonders for the dead? Will the shades arise to give you thanks? Do they declare your kindness in the grave, your faithfulness among those who have perished? Are your wonders made known in the darkness, or your justice in the land of oblivion? (Ps 88:11-13 NAB)

Besides living in covenant with both one's people and the Lord God and praising the God of the Covenant, earthly destiny included the vocation of co-dominion and co-stewardship of the human person with the Creator:

God blessed them, saying: "Be fertile and multiply; fill the earth and subdue it. Have dominion. . . ." God also said: "See, I give you every seed-bearing plant . . . and every tree. . . . " (Gen 1:28-29 NAB).

The Lord God then took the man (*adam*) and settled him in the garden of Eden, to cultivate and care for it (Gen 2:15 NAB).

[And the Lord God] brought them to the man (*adam*) to see what he would call them (animals and birds created by God); whatever he called each of them would be its name (Gen 2:19 NAB).

The created order was not perceived by Israel in the same way as it was in many of the ancient Near-Eastern cultures, that is, as a threatening environment and a place of dreary toil for humans as slaves of the gods. No, the created order was seen as basically good even if it suffered under the curse of human disobedience or sin and the influence of evil:

And so it happened. God looked at everything he had made, and he found it very good (Gen 1:31 NAB).

There shall always be rejoicing and happiness in what I create (Isa 65:18 NAB).

Ancient Israel's neighbors saw the cause or causes of death as coming from without, that is, from outside their biological existence and even from outside earthly existence. Various demons, ghosts, or spirits could cause death or conditions leading to death. The fickleness of the gods presented a danger of death. And among the pantheon of gods there was usually a specific god of death, e.g., the Canaanite god *Mot.*

Unlike their neighbors, ancient Israel sensed that death came from within. They did not understand in a modern sense the biological deterioration of the body, but they did sense that the body had its specific time of natural existence: "Seventy is the sum of our years, or eighty, if we are strong" (Ps 90:10 NAB). At the most, some might live to be over one hundred. But they estimated quite accurately that the biological timetable would not exceed 120 years: "Then the Lord said: 'My spirit shall not abide in mortals forever, for they are flesh; their days shall be one hundred twenty years'" (Gen 6:3 NRSV). They had a sense that God sustained life by that spirit we have spoken of, breathing it into the human being. And long life was a blessing from God. But death was to be accepted as a natural part of life and of existence: "There is . . . a time to be born, and a time to die" (Qoh 3:2 NAB).

Though Israel hoped for a long survival and believed that there was a kind of immortality through one's descendants and in one's name being remembered, they did not ever hold to an annihilation of the human spirit at death, its total destruction. From the most ancient times, they believed that something remained after death, something survived.

Chapter Four
Human Fate after Death in Ancient Israel

"Let me know, O Lord, my end. . . . And now, for what do I wait, O Lord?" (Ps 39:5, 8 NAB) The ancient Israelites, like most persons throughout history, wondered about their fate and life's end and what might exist after death. In the earliest history of Israelite thought, there was less wondering about the questions of afterlife than affirmation of this life as gift, this in contrast to many of the neighboring cultures. Yet, since the beginning of Israelite written experience, there was a belief that something survived death. Early in written revelation, that *something* seemed to be a kind of "double" of the person existing after death, a shadow or shade of the once-living person, someone without vitality (cf. Ps 88:3-5, 1-12 or Isa 14:10, 38:18-19; shades in Hebrew are *rephaim*, cf. Isa 26:19b). Very early, the place of that afterlife existence was called Sheol. It was viewed, as we have seen, as a pit or underworld of not the most pleasant qualities. There is little or nothing known of the etymology of Sheol. There are thirty other references which often substitute for it (e.g., pit, exile, prison, grave).

Moses speculates about the Lord bringing defeat and death to the enemy as proof of Moses' divine mission, and in that one can see an ancient conception of natural mortality and the afterlife:

> If these people die a natural death or if a natural fate comes on them, then the Lord has not sent me. But if the Lord creates something

> new, and the ground opens its mouth and swallows them up, with all that belongs to them, and they go down alive into Sheol, then you shall know. . . . (Num 16:29-30 NRSV)

The Psalms and Proverbs, too, at times share this conception:

> Let not . . . the abyss swallow me up, nor the pit close its mouth over me (Ps 69:16 NAB).

> Let us swallow them up, as the nether world does, alive, in the prime of life, like those who go down to the pit! (Prov 1:12 NAB)

Accepted was a sense of identity which perdured beyond the grave into the afterlife, even in Sheol, as reflected in Psalm 143:3, 7 (NAB):

> He has left *me* dwelling in the dark, like those long dead.

> Hide not your face from me lest I become like those who go down into the pit.

This early identification of an afterlife involved a weak kind of existence. By intertestamental times and during the time that the Greek portions of the Old Testament were written, this existence was given ever-greater attention.

The early revelation wanted to see the dead as buried persons. The dead were seen as ending in one of two places—their own tomb or the common dwelling place of all the dead. Burial was considered the customary and right way of disposing of the dead. Even if a guilty person dies by capital punishment, this custom is to be fulfilled:

> If a man guilty of a capital offense is put to death and his corpse hung on a tree, it shall not remain on the tree overnight. You shall bury it the same day; otherwise, since God's curse rests on him who hangs on a tree, you will defile the land. . . . (Deut 21:22-23 NAB).

Qoheleth could speak of the vanity of life's blessings if a person were denied proper burial: "if . . . [a man] is deprived of burial, of this man I proclaim that the child born dead is more fortunate than he" (6:3 NAB).

The woman Rizpah embarrassed David into giving proper burial to Saul's bones and to the remains of his dead descendants:

> He went and obtained the bones of Saul and of his son Jonathan. . . . the bones of those who had been dismembered were also gathered up. [They] were buried in the tomb of his father Kish at Zela in the territory of Benjamin. After all the king commanded had been carried out, God granted relief to the land (2 Sam 21:12-14 NAB).

There are various texts indicating the importance of owning a family tomb or burial site:

> Abraham buried his wife Sarah in the cave of the field of Machpelah . . . the field . . . transferred . . . to Abraham as a burial place (Gen 23:19-20 NAB).

> Death came to Rebekah's nurse Deborah; she was buried under the oak below Bethel (Gen 35:8 NAB).

> After a full life, he died as an old man and was taken to his kinsmen . . . [who] . . . buried him (Gen 35:29 NAB).

> Samuel was buried at his home in Ramah (1 Sam 25:1 NAB).

Jacob did not wish to be buried in Egypt but wanted to be placed in the tomb of his ancestors. "Do not let me be buried in Egypt. When I lie down with my ancestors, have me taken out of Egypt and buried in their burial place" (Gen 47:29-30 NAB). Joseph, too, wanted his bones to be in the land of his ancestors:

> You must bring my bones up with you from this place (Egypt) (Gen 50:25 NAB).

> Joseph died . . . [and] was embalmed and laid to rest in a coffin in Egypt (Gen 50:26 NAB).

> Ahithophel . . . hanged himself. And so he died and was buried in his father's tomb' (2 Sam 17:23 NAB; cf. 2 Sam 21 above also).

> Judas and his men went to gather up the bodies of the slain and bury them with their kinsmen in their ancestral tombs (2 Macc 12:39 NAB).

It was normal for a person to be buried in the "tomb of his father" (cf. Judg 8:32, 16:31; 2 Sam 2:32, 17:23). The expressions "to sleep with one's fathers" and "to be reunited with one's own," which recorded the deaths of great Old Testament figures, patriarchs, and kings of Israel or Judah, perhaps referred originally to this custom of a family tomb. But the original meaning later took on a deeper sense, and the words became a solemn formula signifying death, and at the same time emphasizing that the ties of blood reached beyond the grave.

The common dwelling place indicated by a shared tomb or gravesite evolved out of and extended to a sense of a general common dwelling of all the dead in Sheol. So Jacob mourned, "I will go down to my son mourning, to Sheol" (Gen 37:35 NAB). Isaiah's taunt-song indicates community: "The nether world below is all astir. . . . It awakens the shades to greet you, all the leaders of the earth" (14:9 NAB). So, too, does Ezekiel's allegory indicate this common dwelling: "For all of them are destined for death, for the land below, for the company of mortals, those who go down into the pit" (31:14 NAB). Sometimes there was an overlapping or acceptance of both situations in one personage. Jacob asked to be buried with his ancestors (47:30 NAB) and yet announced earlier that taking away his last son would send "my white head down to the nether world in grief" (44:29 NAB).

Though Sheol in early times was never given much praise as a place or situation after death, being properly buried or going to the tomb did occasionally bring a pleasant reflection. Job, wishing for the tranquillity of death, groaned:

> For then I should have lain down and been tranquil (Job 3:13 NAB).

> A great anxiety has God allotted and a heavy yoke to the sons of men; From the day one leaves his mother's womb to the day he returns to the mother of all the living, His thoughts, the fear in his heart and his troubled forebodings till the day he dies. . . . (Sir 40:1 RNAB).

> Remember your creator in the days of your youth, before the days of trouble come, and the years draw near when you will say, "I have

no pleasure in them"; . . . because all must go to their eternal home, and the mourners go about the streets (Qoh 12:1, 5b also known as Ecclesiastes, NRSV).

In summary, though there was a definite sense of some kind of afterlife, in the larger portion of the Old Testament this afterlife was from early times understood to lack any of the higher goods or values of a quality life. There was a lack of feelings (cf. Qoh 9:6 NAB), quality knowledge (Qoh 9:10), even lack of memory among the dead, and a lack of remembrance of the dead among the living (cf. Ps 6:6; 31:13; Job 7:7).

One of the worst laments was that one could not give praise to God there or give thanks (cf. Ps 6:5; Bar 2:17; Isa 38:18-19):

> Do you work wonders for the dead? Do the shades rise up to praise you? Is your steadfast love declared in the grave, or your faithfulness in the realm of the dead? Are your wonders known in the darkness, or your saving help in the land of forgetfulness? (Ps 88:10-13 NRSV).

This is, as we have seen, a result of being separated from the covenanted community of the living who were in relationship with the Lord God Yahweh: "The living, the living, give thanks to you, as I do this day" (Isa 38:19 NAB).

Another Israelite custom unique to their religion was the de-mystification of the dead. In the ancient world, a number of societies divinized their ancestors, especially their rulers, after they died. The Romans and Egyptians were well known for this. The ancient Israelites did not make gods of their dead. The religion of "Yahwism" forbade tithing to the dead (Deut 26:14), consulting the dead (necromancy) through mediums (Lev 19:31; 1 Sam 28:3; Deut 26:14),* or even touching the dead (Lev 19:26-28, 31; Deut 18:9-14). Even to touch a corpse accidentally rendered the person "unclean" according to the prophet Haggai, writing after the re-

---

*A difficult text is Isaiah 8:19. It is a mocking reference to necromancy wherein some Israelites must have at one time sought the dead (*mētím*) to speak to them.

turn from the Exile, around 520 B.C.E. (Hag 2:13-14, cf. end of footnote 2 to see exceptions in popular stories so that people could get around these prescriptions). In fact, the idea of the separation of the living from the dead was strong in ancient Israel, and a great deal of impurity was associated both with persons or with cooking pots and other utensils which came in contact with corpses. However, there were rites of purification for undoing such contacts (cf. Lev 11:24-35).

The emphasis on this separation acknowledged that the Lord God was the One with power and influence over life; the dead did not have an influence or power then over life. God was the Lord of history and of his people, and the dead could not change the outcome of history nor have any undue influence over the living. In this particular theological understanding, many ideas of the neighboring cultures were rejected.

There are only a few allusions in the Old Testament about the treatment of the corpse for burial.[12] The custom of closing the eyes of the dead is alluded to in Genesis 46:4. This may have been an almost universal custom and is perhaps simply explained by the resemblance of death to sleep. It seems the nearest relatives would embrace the body (cf. Gen 50:1). In some manner, the body was probably prepared for burial though we have no specific reference to it until the New Testament. Possibly oils and ointments were used in treatment of the bodies. The pins and ornaments found in excavated sites show that the dead were buried fully clothed. Samuel came up from Sheol with his cloak around him (cf. 1 Sam 28:14), and Ezekiel 32:27 tells us that soldiers were laid to rest in their armour, with their swords under their heads and their shields under their bodies.

With the exception of the embalming of Jacob and Joseph according to Egyptian custom (Gen 50:26), embalming was

---

[12]For more information on the treatment of the corpse and burial cf. De Vaux, op cit, 57–60.

never practiced in Israel. The corpse was carried on a bier (cf. 2 Sam 3:31; Luke 7:14) but was not placed in a coffin (cf. 2 Kgs 13:21). Burial probably took place on the day of death since there was no embalming. This is still a custom followed in the East. Though the precept of Deuteronomy 21:22-23 concerns the bodies of those who had been executed (they had to be removed before nightfall), we can presume that the interval between death and burial was very short.

Corpses were not cremated by the Israelites in Canaan from the evidence we possess. In fact, to burn a body was an outrage inflicted only on notorious criminals (cf. Gen 38:24; Lev 20:14; 21:9). One is not to confuse with cremation the references given in Jeremiah 34:5, 2 Chronicles 16:14 or 21:19, which speak of a fire being lit at the death of a king who died at peace with God. This is certainly not cremation, but incense and perfumes which were burned near the body. However, there is one difficult instance—the people of Yabesh in Gilead burnt the bodies of Saul and his sons before burying their bones (cf. 1 Sam 31:12). It seems to have been a departure from traditional usage, and the parallel passage in 1 Chronicles 10:12 omits this point.

From the evidence of excavations, we know that the normal type of Israelite tomb is a burial chamber dug out of soft rock, or one making use of a natural cave. A narrow passage forms the entry and along the inside three sides or walls are ledges on which the bodies were laid. Sometimes there would be an antechamber in larger tombs.[13] Often bones were put in a side cavity, a repository, to make room for new burials. This would be the custom for clan tombs or those held in the family for generations. There does not seem to have been any fixed rule about the position of the bodies. Some per-

[13]Professor Gabriel Barkay, Israeli archeologist, noted in a lecture, February, 1992, for a BAS Seminar, that though the reason for the antechamber remains unclear, one could speculate that it was used for final preparation of a body before it was laid on a shelf or ledge. Or if a family death occurred within days or weeks of another family burial, the stench of decay would be too great in an inner chamber so an antechamber would be needed for a proximate resting place.

sonal belongings and pottery, such as a vase or lamp, were sometimes put beside the corpse. Even gold, silver, and bronze have been found in some burial chambers around Jerusalem. These funeral offerings seemed to become less common as further development in ancient Israelite thought about the fate of the dead occurred.

Since there were families who could not afford the expense of owning and maintaining such tombs, some people were simply laid to rest in the ground. Such is the case in the Kedron Valley near Jerusalem where there was a "tomb of the sons of the people," a kind of poor person's grave. It was a common trench where the bodies of "stateless persons" and condemned criminals were thrown (cf. Jer 26:23; 2 Kgs 23:6).

The necropolis of the kings of Judah, where possibly David and his successors until Ahaz were buried, lay inside the extended ramparts of the city (cf. 1 Kgs 2:10, 11:43, 14:31).

The site of a tomb might be marked by a pillar. Jacob set up a stele (a narrow upright stone with an inscription or writing on it) over Rachel's tomb (Gen 35:20), and Absalom, who had no son "to make his name remembered," had a stele prepared for himself near Jerusalem (cf. 2 Sam 18:18). These may have been early funeral monuments or just memorial columns. It is held that the construction of a monument over the tomb or in connection with it is a late practice. The first written mention of it occurs in connection with the tomb of the Maccabees in Modin (cf. 1 Macc 13:27, 30). The tombs in the Kedron Valley which have monuments over them (so called tombs of Absalom, Josaphat, St. James, and Zacharias) all date from the second or first century B.C.E. or first century C.E. (A.D.).

Though some of the kings were buried within the ramparts and therefore within town, there is no evidence that other dead were buried inside the towns. The tombs were scattered over the surrounding slopes or grouped in places where the nature of the soil was favorable. Often archeologists determine the size of the city by the frame of burial sites surrounding it.

The Israelites mourned their deceased relatives or loved leaders. Those present at the death and funeral went through a certain ritual, as did the close relatives. At the news of death, the first action was to tear one's garments (cf. Gen 37:34; 2 Sam 1:11, 3:31, 13:31; Job 1:20). Then sackcloth was put on (Gen 37:34; 2 Sam 3:31). It was a coarse material, usually worn next to the skin, around the waist and below the breast (cf. 2 Kgs 6:30; 2 Macc 3:19). The mourners took off their shoes (cf. 2 Sam 15:30; Ezek 24:17, 23; Mic 1:8). Men covered their beards (Ezek 24:17, 23) or veiled their faces (cf. 2 Sam 19:5, 15:30). Scripture speaks of the expression of sorrow or shame being the gesture of putting one's hands on one's head, but it also was probably used in mourning (cf. 2 Sam 13:19; Jer 2:37).

The mourner would also put earth on his head (cf. Josh 7:6; 1 Sam 4:12; Neh 9:1; 2 Macc 10:25, 14:15; Job 2:12; Ezek 27:30). That person would roll his head (Job 16:15) or even his whole body (Mic 1:10) in the dust, and lie or sit among a heap of ashes (cf. Esth 4:3; Isa 58:5; Jer 6:26; Ezek 27:30). Mourners refrained from using perfumes (2 Sam 12:20, 14:2; Jud 10:3).

In Leviticus 19:27-28, 21:5, and Deuteromony 14:1, such rites as cutting one's body and shaving hair and beards were condemned as preserving heathen rites.

The usual period of strict mourning where there often was fasting was seven days (cf. 1 Sam 31:13; Gen 50:10; Jud 16:24; Sir 22:12).

Friends and neighbors brought mourning bread and the "cup of consolation" to the relatives of the deceased, for the uncleanness which was attached to the house of the dead prevented food from being prepared there (Jer 16:7; Ezek 24:17, 22; Hos 9:4).

The lamentation for the dead was the chief funeral ceremony. In its simplest form it was a sharp, repeated cry, compared in Micah 1:8 to the call of the jackal or the ostrich. For the death of an only son, the lamentation was particularly heartrending (cf. Jer 6:26; Amos 8:10; Zech 12:10). These cries of the mourners were uttered by the men and women in separate groups (Zech 12:11-14). Lamenting was the duty of close relations, though everyone present joined in since to "make mourning" means "to perform the lamentation" (Gen 23:2, 50:10; 1 Sam 25:1, 28:3; 2 Sam 1:11-12, 19-27, 3:31, 33-34, 11:26). Often these laments were composed and sung by professionals, men or women, and were then taught to their daughters (2 Chr 35:25; Amos 5:16; Jer 9:16f; Ezek 32:16). It seemed that these rites formed a part of what children did to honor their parents as enjoined by the Decalogue (Ten Commandments). The dead were honored in a religious spirit, but no cult was paid to them.

Sometimes the laments for individuals were used to depict the misfortunes of Israel or its kings or its enemies. One of the finest examples is the Book of Lamentations (cf. also Jer 9:9-11, 16-21; Ezek 19:1-14, 26:17-18, 27:2-9, 25-36, 28:12-19; Amos 5:1-2).

With the progression of history and individual consciousness among the Israelites, in addition to several large-scale defeats of the people in the Babylonian conquest and exile and later the subjugation under the Greeks (587 B.C.E.—Babylonians, 350–160 B.C.E.—Greeks), addressing the question of the afterlife became more demanding. A theological reflection emerged from some long-held and long-asked questions. Basically, the questions centered around the strong desire to know something more of the destiny of a person who enjoyed intimacy both with God in this life and with God's community of Israel. Would not the faithfulness of God allow a continued spiritual enjoyment of intimacy in the afterlife? There was also the enduring question of God's justice in relation to the conduct of human beings. If humans do not experience God's justice in regard to the good or the wicked in this life, will justice not then take place in the afterlife to make things right? There was anxiety when a vacuum of justice was sensed, for people observed that many died not having experienced divine justice in relation to their covenant response to God or in relation to their conduct.

During the long first period of Israelite religion, there was a sense that God's justice and the need for retribution would be in relation to the community and take place in the community. Thus the classic pronouncement of Exodus 34:6-7, which saw conduct being rewarded or punished in the descendants of a person, in successive generations. Psalm 1 is an ancient classical plea that sinners be punished now and the just rewarded in the community in this life. Psalms 54 and 69 pray for retribution, an early understanding of how it should take place in this life.

In the second period of Israelite religion, a number of places can be found in the body of Revelation accenting individual retribution in opposition to corporate or descendant retribution. Human beings during this period of time were beginning to experience themselves not only as part of a corporate identity, but differentiated in their own self-consciousness as separate or individual identities:

> The fathers shall not be put to death for the children, nor shall the children be put to death for the fathers; everyone shall be put to death for his own sin (Deut 24:16 NRSV).

> In those days they shall no longer say: "The fathers have eaten sour grapes, and the children's teeth are set on edge." But every one shall die for his own sin (Jer 31:29-30 NRSV; cf. all of Ezek 18; Prov 11:21).

This heightened sense of individual retribution or justice sharpened the observation among the Israelites that the equation often did not work: that is, the wicked were not always punished and the innocent were not always left unharmed. Yet they professed that God was just. So where and when would the appropriate fairness or justice happen? At first, the mystery was left in God's hands, so to speak. Then, the inspiration that justice would surely happen in the afterlife began to be shared and accepted. With this inspiration came a faith not only in an afterlife lived in the presence of God but also a belief in a final justification or judgment from God.

The Books of Job and Qoheleth (Ecclesiastes) are sometimes called anti-Wisdom Books or contestational wisdom in that they confronted the traditional wisdom that retribution and reward must happen in this life. That traditional wisdom is expressed in the question of Eliphaz in his argument with Job:

> Think now, who that was innocent ever perished? Or where were the upright cut off? As I have seen, those who plow iniquity and sow trouble reap the same (Job 4:7-8 NRSV).

This wisdom eventually became unconvincing as both Job and Qoheleth observed some of the wicked prospering and some of the innocent suffering terribly. So Job looks for another answer. And Qoheleth takes refuge in cynicism as he challenges the presumptions of former wisdom.

A developing answer in Revelation affirmed the Lord God Yahweh as just judge, savior, and source of hope in face of the mystery of this life's injustice:

> There is not a just and saving God but me. Turn to me and be safe. . . . In the Lord shall be the vindication and the glory of all the descendants of Israel (Isa 45:21-22, 25 NRSV).

And the power to save and the content of saving is affirmed in the question the Lord God asks:

> Shall I deliver them from the power of the nether world? Shall I redeem them from death? Where are your plagues, O death! Where is your sting, O nether world! (Hos 13:14 NAB).

> He shall destroy death forever (Isa 25:8 NAB).

God's justice in the afterlife may be hinted at in 1 Samuel 2:6: "The Lord . . . brings down to Sheol and brings up." In Job 33:29, Scripture continues:

> God indeed does all these things, twice, three times, with mortals, to bring back their souls from the Pit, so that they may see the light of life (NRSV).

> Walk in the ways of your heart and the sight of your eyes. But know that for all these things God will bring you into judgment (Qoh 11:9 NAB).

The last verse of Qoheleth expresses his faith, and trusts the mystery of God's justice: "For God will bring every deed into judgment, with every secret thing, whether good or evil" (Qoh 12:14). Job finally protests and confirms his faith in the ultimate vindication in God, "But as for me, I know that my Vindicator (another translation has 'Redeemer') lives, and that he will at last stand forth upon the dust" (Job 19:25).

It is estimated that during the Persian and early Greek period (500–200 B.C.E.) of Israelite history, a distinct insight and revelation of a resurrection of the just began to develop. The idea of resurrection was not new in itself, for ancient neighbors of Israel had had resurrections of gods and goddesses for a long time, such as Osiris (Egyptian), Tammuz (Babylonian), and Adonis (Greek).

In contradistinction to these neighbors, Israel's development related to humans in a covenant relationship with God and included the unique insight of a reward in the afterlife being inclusive of the resurrection of the just. Earlier mysterious scriptural texts about Enoch and Elijah were seen in a new light and as support for this new hope in reward, resurrection, and community with the Lord God in the afterlife:

> Enoch walked with God, and he was no longer here, for God took him (Gen 5:24 NAB).

> "Still, if you see me taken up from you, your wish will be granted; otherwise not." As they walked on conversing, a flaming chariot and flaming horses came between them, and Elijah went up to the heavens in a whirlwind (2 Kgs 2:10-11 NAB).

Thus Sirach took over these events in the words he wrote with further interpretation:

> You (Elijah) were taken aloft in a whirlwind, in a chariot with fiery horses. You were destined, it is written, in time to come to put an end to wrath before the day of the Lord (48:9-10 NAB).

> Few on earth have been made the equal of Enoch, for he was taken up bodily (49:14 NAB).

During the Greek period (sometimes known, too, as the Seleucid or the Ptolemaic period) the Jews experienced persecution both of their culture and their religion. Early in this epoch, Daniel's work was completed. Though Daniel does not have a precise doctrine of the afterlife, he does proclaim the new strand of belief and insight about resurrection. This reward may have been limited to certain chosen Israelites and does not make a clear distinction between a resurrection on this earth or a resurrection to heaven. In relation to this, we have the often-quoted line of Daniel:

> Many of those who sleep in the dust of the earth shall awake, some shall live forever, others shall be an everlasting horror and disgrace. But the wise shall shine brightly like the splendor of the firmament, and those who lead the many to justice, shall be like the stars forever (12:2-3 RNAB).

In any event, the resurrection here was restricted to the just while the wicked were left in dark oblivion, their memory a horror and disgrace. In the Hebrew canon, it is only in the Book of Daniel where the happy reward of the saints and the resurrection of their bodies appear clearly. Later writings in Greek affirming the resurrection and a fuller afterlife were incorporated into the Christian canon of Old Testament books.

Later in this period, during the Maccabean epoch of persecution (ca. 180–120 B.C.E.), a doctrine of afterlife seemed well accepted in this group of zealous and patriotic Israelites whereby the Lord God Yahweh would reward a faithful life. In the story of a mother and her seven sons during the persecution, we have the second of the martyred sons saying at the point of death, "You are depriving us of this present life, but the king of the world will raise us up to live again forever" (2 Macc 7:9 NAB).

When the third son was asked if he would renounce his faith, "he boldly held out his hands, and said courageously: 'The God of heaven gave me these. His laws mean far more to me than they do, and it is from him that I trust to receive them back'" (2 Macc 7:12 translation author's). The fourth son said at the point of death, "It is my choice to die at the hands of men with the God-given hope of being restored to life by him; but for you, there will be no resurrection to life" (7:14).

The mother encouraged each son with these words:

> Since it is the Creator of the universe who shapes each one's beginning, as he brings about the origin of everything, God, in his mercy, will give you back both breath and life because you disregard yourselves for the sake of his law (7:23 translation author's).

A final reference to resurrection in 2 Maccabees says:

> [Judas] took up a collection. . . . He sent to Jerusalem to provide for an expiatory sacrifice. In doing this he acted in a very excellent and noble way, inasmuch as he had the resurrection of the dead in view; for if he were not expecting the fallen to rise again, it would have been useless and foolish to pray for them in death. But if he did this with a view to the splendid reward that awaits those who had gone to rest in godliness, it was a holy and pious thought (12:43-45 translation author's).

One would label most of these references to hope in the resurrection "apocalyptic hope" which arose during times of persecution. At times, this strand is found in the major prophets such as Ezekiel, Deutero-Isaiah, and Daniel, or in the Psalms. For instance, we have in Isaiah:

> But your dead shall live, their corpses shall rise; awake and sing, you who lie in the dust. For your dew is a dew of light and the land of shades gives birth (26:19 NAB).

> He will revive us after two days; on the third day he will raise us up, to live in his presence (Hos 6:2 NAB).

Although these passages may only refer to a kind of resuscitation, they prepared minds to accept the possibility of new

life after death. Thus in Psalm 49:16 we read, "God will re-
deem me from the power of the nether world by receiving
me." However, this strand of hope in the resurrection is
found especially in the Books of the Maccabees.

Later—in late Wisdom for instance, such as the Wisdom
of Solomon, written perhaps in the late second century before Christ—it seems there is more than the apocalyptic present. Whether or not something dramatic would happen by
God's intervention in this world, there was a sense of immortality beyond this earth. There seems to be a further development of revelation:

> For God formed man to be imperishable; the image of his own na-
> ture he made him (2:23 RNAB).

> But the just one, though he die early, shall be at rest (4:7).

> His soul was pleasing to the Lord, therefore he sped him out of
> the midst of wickedness (4:14).

> Yes, the just dead condemns the sinful who live, and youth swiftly
> completed condemns the many years of the wicked grown old (4:16).

The Book of Wisdom insists throughout on the immortality
of the human person: "Their hope is full of immortality"
(3:4); "The souls of the just are in the hand of God" (3:1).

One can observe in this late Old Testament development
a shift in attitude toward early death—that is, a less-than-full
natural life—from being a tragedy to being a blessing if early
death resulted from holding fast to the Law or to the faith,
or was a release from further suffering involved in persecution or ill-fortune.

This development, though an emerging strong current of
thought, did not displace an older, more traditional view of
natural human mortality. Thus, side by side with the Book
of Wisdom and from close to the same era in history, one
can find in the Book of Sirach:

> No more can the dead give praise than those who have never lived;
> they glorify the Lord who are alive and well (17:23 NAB).

God watches over the hosts of highest heaven, while all men are dust and ashes (17:27 NAB).

Whether one has lived a thousand years, a hundred, or ten, in the nether world he has no claim on life (41:4 NAB).

These two divergent currents of thought were representatively held by two late Old Testament sects, the Pharisees and the Sadducees. The Sadducees categorically rejected the resurrection of the dead and immortality of the soul as found in Matthew 22:23 and in Acts 23:8. In Acts 23:8 we have a summary of Pharisaic belief in the resurrection, in angels, and in spirits.

There was a sectarian, ascetic community living by the Dead Sea at a place called Qumran from the first century B.C.E. until the Romans crushed them around 70 C.E. (A.D.). They were called the Essenes and had removed themselves from Jerusalem society to await and prepare themselves for the Day of the Lord and God's mighty intervention. They held a belief in some form of afterlife and resurrection of the dead. These are difficult texts (the excavated Qumran Scrolls) which probably did not hold to any resurrection of the body (which they held to be corrupt) rather, they held to a belief in a resurrection of the soul or spirit of the person.

Apart from some of the sects' various beliefs, there was a popular piety which for centuries passed on the stories about saintly persons, such as Enoch or Elijah, who were taken up from earth to be bodily alive with God (cf. Gen 5:24; 2 Kgs 2:11). This piety must have seen the body as a dignified part of God's plan, not only for this earth but in the afterlife as well. Elisha's body, for instance, could not be considered unclean if the corpse of a man, hurriedly lowered into the same grave, "came back to life and rose to his feet" upon "contact with the bones of Elisha" (2 Kgs 13:21). By this faith in life beyond this earth, belief in the resurrection eventually dawned.

Therefore, we come into New Testament times with several simultaneous currents of thought about the afterlife. At this point, we turn to the New Testament to study the further development of revelation concerning the death and destiny of humans revealed through the Christian development of the Bible.

Chapter Five
Death and Destiny
in the New Testament

Introduction

The New Testament has often been seen by many people as a completely new teaching. However, after studying the Old Testament, both the Hebrew writings and the Greek portions, one can observe that New Testament revelation takes currents of thought in previous revelation writings and develops them. Immortality, which was a concept and belief present as revelation both in the late Old Testament and in Greek Gentile thought, is distinctly and unanimously affirmed. Reward and punishment, the differentiation of the good from the wicked in the afterlife, is confirmed. A causal connection between sin and mortality will be more confidently asserted. Resurrection of the dead is defined as resurrection of the body as well. And finally, anticipation of the afterlife, especially heaven and union with God, is encouraged in the New Testament. In the meantime, the books therein do not neglect a commitment to this life. Participation in eternal life as a quality of this life will be introduced in the New Testament and is especially pronounced in the Gospel and writings of John.

Despite these developments, the New Testament leaves much for further clarification. There are questions which readers will continually pose, such as those concerning the nature of heaven or hell, or the in-between state of existence for humans awaiting the final judgment at the end of the world, or resurrection of the dead. There remains the nagging question of God's justice (theodicy) being fulfilled in this life, or in an in-between state before final judgment, that is, somehow in the afterlife. Also, many might wonder—because of certain passages—whether there is ongoing growth in God's grace through death and for a period after death, whereby God continues to perfect the human creature. These questions are not given clear answers in our texts. However, one may sense some trajectories out of the texts whereby the Christian Church has later presented clearer answers from its traditions.

Central to New Testament thought is the resurrection of Jesus. It became a reality perceived as something far more than resuscitation and even more than an end in itself for humans. Resurrection, after Jesus' own resurrection, was now seen as a renewal of creation and also of the community of faithful believers. The fearfulness of death for Christians is muted by the perception that its power has been broken by the resurrection of Jesus, who continues to empower his followers. The various writers of the New Testament, as the starting point for their words and writing, have this fact of their faith and this hope which became the revelation held by Christians. Paul spoke of that shared hope in Romans 6:8f:

> If we have died with Christ, we believe that we are also to live with him. We know that Christ, once raised from the dead, will never die again; death has no more power over him (NAB).

In the light of this definitive revelation of the resurrection, let us first summarize the attitude toward life in the New Testament. Later, we can observe the developing view of the afterlife. The emphasis of the New Testament is far and away so centered on the promise and hope of eternal life that one must search long and hard to find texts explicitly holding up this life as a wonderful gift to be lived. One could assert that the witness of Jesus and the Spirit implicitly affirms the gift of this life in the body. The incarnation in its very nature blesses the material world, and all that God created, as good. Paul urged in the earliest of his writings (50–55 C.E.) that Christians respect labor and occupy themselves with doing good, praying, rejoicing, and being at peace:

> Be at peace among yourselves. And we exhort you, brethren, admonish the idlers, encourage the fainthearted, help the weak, be patient with them all. See that none of you repays evil for evil, but always seek to do good to one another and to all. Rejoice always, pray constantly, give thanks in all circumstances (1 Thess 5:13-18 NAB).

And later, in 2 Thessalonians 3:7-10, Paul urges his readers to occupy themselves with useful work:

> For you yourselves know how you ought to imitate us; we were not idle when we were with you, we did not eat anyone's bread without paying, but with toil and labor we worked night and day, that we might not burden any of you. . . . If anyone will not work, let him not eat (NAB).

The Scriptures had long ago rejected the notion of work as slavery to the gods, as we have seen in the summary from the Old Testament. The Old Testament notion of being stewards of God's creation and co-caretakers, exercising dominion, and doing purposeful work, is preserved in the New Testament. Jesus speaks of that attitude of co-worker in John 5:17: "My Father is working still, and I am working."

Jesus sensed, as did the early Christian, that there was a definite purposeful work given to each person. And thus he could include in his prayer in John 17 a confirmation of that work completed. In verse 4 he says, "I glorified you on earth, having accomplished the work which you gave me to do." Paul advised living the life the Lord has assigned: "Let every one lead the life which the Lord has assigned to him, and in which God has called him" (1 Cor 7:17 RSV). That life was a duty of work was strongly felt; it was seen as an imitation of God's creative work during the six days of creation.

Thus a synagogue ruler could say, "There are six days on which work ought to be done . . . [but] not on the sabbath day" (Luke 13:14 RSV).

Strong in the Jewish tradition, and reaffirmed in the Christian tradition, was the notion of doing good to others and doing it in this world. In the late letter to Titus, we hear the advice:

> I desire you to insist on these things so that those who have believed in God may be careful to apply themselves to good deeds (an alternate manuscript reads "enter honorable occupations"); these are excellent and profitable to men (3:8 RSV).

> And let our people learn to apply themselves to good deeds, so as to help cases of urgent need, and not to be unfruitful (3:14 RSV).

The Christian influence on the tradition was to emphasize that the work of life should be work in the Lord, and for the Lord, and even be work toward salvation:

> Therefore, my beloved brethren, be steadfast, immovable, always abounding in the work of the Lord, knowing that in the Lord your labor is not in vain (1 Cor 15:58 RSV).

> Whatever your task, work heartily, as serving the Lord and not men, knowing that from the Lord you will receive the inheritance as your reward; you are serving the Lord Christ (Col 3:23 RSV).

> Whatever you do, do all to the glory of God (1 Cor 10:31 RSV).

> Work out your own salvation with fear and trembling; for God is at work in you, both to will and to work for his good pleasure (Phil 2:12-13 RSV).

By encouraging work for the glory of God and for the welfare of others, one can deduce that life was accepted as a gift and a responsibility. In this sense, life was welcomed, and guidelines throughout the New Testament tell us how to live with gusto, purpose, and in love and peace. Yet, for all this, the predominant theme of the New Testament concerning life is that it is highly transitory and a preparation for eternal life. Christ's resurrection radically redirected humanity toward another qualitatively richer and infinite life. Therefore, Paul could say, "If for this life only we have hoped in Christ, we are the most pitiable people of all" (1 Cor 15:19 RNAB).

The author of the Book of Hebrews, emphasizing that we are but sojourners on earth, recalled the story of Abraham as a sojourner to show that Christians living in faith were part of an older tradition and that even Abraham's hope must have gone beyond this life:

> These all died in faith, not having received what was promised, but having seen it and greeted it from afar, and having acknowledged that they were strangers and exiles on the earth. For people who speak thus make it clear that they are seeking a homeland. If they had been thinking of that land from which they had gone out, they would have had opportunity to return. But as it is, they desire a better country, that is, a heavenly one (11:13-15 NAB).

The letter of James is even more pointed about this life's transitoriness:

> Whereas you do not know about tomorrow, what is your life? For you are a mist that appears for a little time and then vanishes. Instead you ought to say, "If the Lord wills, we shall live and do this or that" (4:14-15 RSV).

In the end, the New Testament does not negate or lessen life in relation to the afterlife, nor vice versa. Paul eloquently emphasizes the unity of this life and the afterlife in the Lord:

> None of us lives as his own master and none of us dies as his own master. While we live we are responsible to the Lord, and when we die we die as his servants. Both in life and death we are the Lord's (Rom 14:7-8 NAB).

That said, however, it does not lessen our earlier observation that the primary emphasis for the Christian was and is to keep eyes focused on the destiny of life's journey—eternal life and union with the Lord.

That life is insecure and transitory continues to be the New Testament theme so that readers and hearers may keep their minds and hearts set on the life that will never end. In Luke 12:19f, Jesus concludes a poignant parable about the rich man and all his harvests:

> "Then I will say to myself: You have blessings in reserve for years to come. Relax! Eat heartily, drink well. Enjoy yourself." But God said to him, "You fool! This very night your life shall be required of you. To whom will all this piled-up wealth of yours go?" (NAB)

Death and Burial

The New Testament contains little on actual burial practices other than a few references which continue the accepted Old Testament custom for bodily burial, usually in hewn tombs in rocky hillsides or in cave-like structures. We can imagine these structures among the heights east of the Sea of Galilee when Jesus was visiting the territory of the Gerasenes. He was met by a man possessed who lived among the tombs (Mark 5:2). When John the Baptist was beheaded, his followers did not leave it to Herod to take care of the body afterward: "They came and took his body, and laid it in a tomb" (Mark 6:29). Part of the scandal of the parable about the death of the son of the owner of the vineyard in Mark 12 was the casting out of his body from the vineyard after he was killed. It presented the picture of a lack of proper burial on one's own land or in one's own country.

Jewish practice was to seal the tomb after burial, usually with a stone put in place to cover the entrance or opening. The mourners wrapped the body in two wrappings, one for the body and one for the head, binding the jaw and facial structure which tends to relax or sag after death:

> Then Jesus, deeply moved again, came to the tomb; it was a cave, and a stone lay upon it. Jesus said, "Take away the stone." Martha, the sister of the dead man, said to him, "Lord, by this time there will be an odor, for he has been dead four days." . . . [Jesus] cried with a loud voice, "Lazarus, come out." The dead man came out, his hands and feet bound with bandages, and his face wrapped

with a cloth. Jesus said to them, "Unbind him, and let him go" (John 11:38-44 RSV).

The most extensive revelation of Jewish burial practices occurs in relation to the burial of Jesus. It seems that not only proper burial in a hewn tomb was important, but so were burial wrappings and anointings:

> Joseph of Arimathea, a respected member of the council . . . went to Pilate, and asked for the body of Jesus. . . . He granted the body to Joseph. And he brought a linen shroud, and laid him in a tomb which had been hewn out of the rock; and he rolled a stone against the door of the tomb. . . . Mary Magdalene, and Mary the mother of James, and Salome, bought spices, so that they might go and anoint him (Mark 15:43–16:1 RSV).

John is more precise about the Jewish custom of wrappings and anointings. The wrappings were linen, and the body was anointed not only with a fragrant oil but also with a special mixture to which spices had been added:

> Nicodemus also . . . came bringing a mixture of myrrh and aloes, about a hundred pounds weight. They took the body of Jesus, and bound it in linen cloths with the spices, as is the burial custom of the Jews (John 19:39-40 RSV).

This custom was accepted by Jesus when he commented on the anointing he received from Mary and on what remained of the very expensive, fragrant nard: "Let her alone, let her keep it for the day of my burial" (John 12:7 RSV).

Burial customs, as developed in the late Old Testament, were carried on as the accepted tradition in the New Testament. The early common reference in the Old Testament to Sheol being the place of the dead as their dwelling has a number of parallels in the New Testament. This could cause us confusion if we are not aware of translation problems, for Sheol became a euphemism for the dead. Yet let us say in passing, the ancient sense of a dwelling place for the dead seems part of the accepted mental furniture of writers of the New Testament.

"Sheol" of the Old Testament was translated as "Hades" in the Septuagint. Thus the word "Hades" was used in the New Testament, its texts being of Greek composition. Frequently, this was translated as "hell" in English texts, without differentiation from the hell of eternal damnation, though this last theme is likewise developed in the New Testament. The hell of eternal damnation is to be differentiated from the concept of Sheol in the Old Testament. On one occasion, the Latin *tartarus* is used as the original word in the text: "God did not spare the angels when they sinned, but cast them into hell (*tartarus*) and committed them to pits of nether gloom to be kept until judgment" (2 Pet 2:4). One can notice that this description is reminiscent of the understanding of Sheol in the Old Testament.

Hades is seemingly not a permanent place but can be a place of visitation, even a temporary stay. This interpretation would need to be accepted in order to read the texts of Acts, for instance, when Peter is preaching of Jesus: "You killed him, but God raised him to life, freeing him from the pangs of hell (read: *Hades*)" (Acts 2:23), or "[Christ] is the one who was not abandoned to hell (*Hades*)" (Acts 2:31).[14] Christ, after his death, visited Sheol or Hades: "In saying, 'He ascended,' what does it mean but that he had also descended into the lower parts of the earth?" (Eph 4:9 RSV) This last reference from Paul is often paired with 1 Peter 3:19 where Christ goes to this place of the dead: "For Christ also died. . . . he went and preached to the spirits in prison" (RSV).

Finally, in the visions of the Book of Revelation, both "death" and "Hades" seem to refer to the same thing, as if they were interchangeable terms: "Death and hell delivered up the dead" (20:13 RSV), and "I am the Living One. I was dead and now I am to live for ever and ever, and I hold the keys of death and of the underworld" (1:17-18).

[14]*Hades* is used in the Western Text Manuscript, but the Textus Receptus uses "of death" which shows the seemingly accepted notion that *Hades* is a euphemism for death or for the dead.

One of the principal purposes of the above summary is to show that the revelation of the New Testament presumes an understanding of the Old Testament and that there was not an absolute schism between the new ideas and what had been revealed or had come to be understood in the previous development of revelation.

Another aspect introduced by the New Testament is the unsettled question about the immediate situation of those who have just died and await the final judgment and the resurrection of the dead. There is a sense of a place of the dead, of waiting, of sleeping, and of longing. Thus we have Revelation 6:9 where the Lamb opened the fifth seal and John saw in a vision that under the altar were souls of those who had been slain for the Word of God and for the witness they had born:

> They cried out with a loud voice, "O Sovereign Lord, holy and true, how long before you will judge and avenge our blood on those who dwell upon the earth?" Then they were each given a white robe and told to rest a little longer (6:10-11 RSV).

In some Christian traditions,[15] this period or state of existence is identified with and incorporated into a reality called purgatory. For others it remains just a mystery, the data of Scripture judged to be incomplete.

In the New Testament, there are various developments of the understanding of death and destiny. The principal developments come in Paul's writings, the Synoptic Gospels (Mark, Matthew, Luke), and John. In the next chapter, we will examine and summarize these presentations.

---

[15]With Catholics, for instance, purgatory is an ancient Christian belief that there is a transitional period or state of purification whereby the grace of God continues to work on perfecting the human subject as a result of the wounds suffered in human nature due to their personal sins. Besides the Scripture employed in the Catholic tradition (cf. Heb 12:23-24; Rev 6:9f; Sir 7:33; 2 Macc 12:38-46; Matt 12:32), a number of early Church Fathers can be quoted as handing on this belief (e.g., Gregory, Ephrem, Cyprian, Ambrose, Chrysostom, Augustine). "You have come to God himself, the supreme Judge, and been placed with the spirits of the saints who have been made perfect" (Heb 12:23). After death, believers become consummately perfected in the Blood of Jesus.

Chapter Six
Death and Destiny in Paul, the Synoptic Gospels, and John

St. Paul

The earliest New Testament writer (ca. 50 C.E.) was Paul. For Paul, the reality of death is far more than a human biological problem or destiny. Death is a metaphor for the effects of evil and sin in the cosmos. So death is a far more pervasive reality for Paul than it was for previous writers. Whereas in Old Testament writings death was first just a reality of life to be accepted, then later symbolically inclusive of that which limited full life (such as illness, persecution, alienation, and worst of all, premature death), for Paul death became a much larger, all-embracing reality.

Death was more than biological dying. Death was more than just separation from the living Israelite community, as in some of the formulations of the Psalms and the covenant formulations in Isaiah. And it was more than just a vexing problem as it was for Qoheleth. Rather, death has the widest metaphoric meaning for Paul, covering everything within creation which deviates from the Creator's design. The material creation itself is seen to be in a state of decay.

There was some hint in Qoheleth 25:24 that premature death, at least, is attributable to human sin or error. But that is now generalized to show how death for humans and for material creation entered the world through human sin back in the Garden of Eden:

Just as through one transgression condemnation came upon all, so through one righteous act acquittal and life came to all. For just as through the disobedience of one person the many were made sinners, so through the obedience of one the many will be made righteous (Rom 5:18-19 RNAB, cf. Rom 8:19-21).

And further on, Paul says, "The wages of sin is death" (6:23). If there has been a rabbinic interpretation of Genesis 2–3 that mortality is part of the Creator's original design regardless of sin, then what is shown here is that death is part of the Creator's design because of human sin. Paul summarized his thought in Romans 5:12: "Therefore, just as through one person sin entered the world, and through sin, death, and thus death came to all . . ." (NAB).

Sin is also, according to Paul, part of God's design (distinguished from the will of God) due to the power and activity of the devil. Paul takes an idea first presented in the Old Testment Book of Wisdom (cf. 2:23, 24) which stated that death entered the world through the devil's spite, and develops and folds it into his presentation of the revelation of the close relation between sin and death.

For Paul, this activity of the devil has infected the world and set it in opposition to God's design:

> For we are not contending against flesh and blood, but against the principalities, against the powers, against the world rulers of this present darkness, against the spiritual hosts of wickedness in the heavenly places (Eph 6:12 NAB).

> Creation was made subject to futility, not of its own accord but by him who once subjected it; yet not without hope, because the world itself will be freed from its slavery to corruption and share in the glorious freedom of the children of God (Rom 8:19-21 NAB).

If mortality is the result of human sin, which was influenced and perpetuated by the devil's activity, then according to Paul the victory over the devil and over sin in one man reversed that process:

> Therefore just as one man's trespass led to condemnation for all, so one man's act of righteousness leads to justification and life for all. For just as by the one man's disobedience the many were made sinners, so by the one man's obedience the many will be made righteous (Rom 5:18-19 RNAB).

And that mortality of the world and of humans is an evil which ultimately will be overcome: "For he (Christ) must reign until he has put all his enemies under his feet. The last enemy to be destroyed is death" (1 Cor 15:25-26 NAB).

The Pauline influence on Christian development focuses on belief in the victory of God over the forces of chaos and death. Death has been defeated, although temporarily it continues to manifest itself biologically. That biological manifestation, too, will cease at the completion of the transition to the new age when the living and the dead will be granted immortality:

> The trumpet will sound and the dead will be raised incorruptible, and we shall be changed. This corruptible body must be clothed with incorruptibility, this mortal body with immortality. When the corruptible frame takes on incorruptibility and the mortal immortality, then will the saying of Scripture be fulfilled: "Death is swallowed up in victory" (1 Cor 15:52b-54 NAB).

Though Paul applies the notion of death to all creation, this does not mean he or the reader of his letters ought to be moribund. Rather, there is cause for rejoicing because of the resurrection of Jesus. Therefore, believers are to perceive the world in a new light and see new possibilities. "Walk in newness of life" (Rom 6:4) is an attitude further reflected in comparing the human origin and destiny of Adam of the Old Testament and the New Adam who is Jesus:

> The first man was from the earth, a man of dust; the second man is from heaven. As was the man of dust, so are those who are of the dust; and as is the man of heaven, so are those who are of heaven. Just as we have borne the image of the man of dust, we shall also bear the image of the man of heaven (1 Cor 15:47-49 NAB).

Ultimately, the possibilities meant more than individual resurrection or the resurrection of all believers; it included the rebirth of the entire world.

Paul's own attitude toward death indicated the Christian hope for becoming a part of an intimate community with Christ and others. The resurrection was seen as far more than a mere grave-emptying operation:

> We know that while we are at home in the body we are away from the Lord. . . . We would rather be away from the body and at home with the Lord. So whether we are at home or away, we make it our aim to please him (2 Cor 5:6-9 NAB).

> Life to me, of course, is Christ, but death would bring me something more; . . . I am caught in this dilemma: I want to be gone and be with Christ, which would be very much better, but for me to stay alive in this world is more urgent for your sake (Phil 1:21-24 JB).*

Death is not seen as an escape to be desired, as so often was the case in Greek or Hellenistic literature. Death, or mortality, was seen as part of the picture of the world passing away, but it has lost its power to negate one's energies. Death has lost its ultimacy.

The Synoptic Gospels

Within the gospels, there is little of the detailed speculation about the nature of life after death which characterized the time of late Old Testament writings. Jesus' own teaching, as is true of the gospels, primarily emphasizes the insecurity and shortness of life. Apart from the few instances of biological death—reports of the death of John the Baptist and the more extended account of Jesus' own death—and his acts of resuscitation of the sick or raising the dead, biological death is primarily alluded to as an incentive to prepare for the impending arrival of the new age:

*These quotations from Paul must have been tied to a personal mystical experience he describes in 2 Corinthians 12:2-3 of being taken to the "third heaven." Paul was not sure of the relation of his body to his spirit at that time. It was extraordinary for Paul to recount such an event and to indicate how words failed him ("words that cannot be uttered") to express the experience.

> In those days came John the Baptist, preaching in the wilderness of Judea, "Repent, for the kingdom of heaven is at hand. . . . Even now the ax is laid to the root of the trees; every tree therefore that does not bear good fruit is cut down and thrown into the fire" (Matt 3:1-2, 10 NAB).

> And he (Jesus) told them a parable, saying, "The land of a rich man brought forth plentifully. . . . And he said, 'I will pull down my barns, and build larger ones.' . . . But God said to him, 'Fool! This night your soul is required of you; and the things you have prepared, whose will they be?' " (Luke 12:16-20 RSV)

Death is not a focus for the Gospels because it has lost its ultimate importance. It has only relative importance compared to the new possibilities revealed about eternal life. Thus Jesus could advise his followers: "Do not fear those who kill the body but cannot kill the soul; rather, fear him (God) who can destroy both soul and body in hell" (Matt 10:28 RSV). This quote fits into the larger context concerning Christian discipleship which involves the all-important regard for God and choice for Jesus rather than for earthly human powers. Nor should reward in this life be much of a concern in relation to the ultimate possibilities: "You should be pleased they cannot repay you, for you will be repaid in the resurrection of the just" (Luke 14:14 NAB).

Luke 14:14 also shows that the future reality of resurrection for the dead is assumed. The teaching of Jesus was explicit about this. We can see it in Mark's Gospel where the Sadducees, who did not believe in the resurrection, try to trip Jesus over the matter of a levirate marriage where the woman would supposedly have seven earthly husbands awaiting her in the afterlife. Their question concerned who would be her real husband in another life. They also posed the question assuming the resurrection meant people coming back to life. Jesus said:

> You are badly misled, because you fail to understand the Scriptures or the power of God. When people rise from the dead, they neither marry nor are given in marriage but live like angels in heaven.

As to the raising of the dead, have you not read in the book of Moses, in the passage about the burning bush, how God told him, "I am the God of Abraham, the God of Isaac, the God of Jacob"? He is the God of the living, not of the dead. You are very much mistaken (Mark 12:24-27 NAB).

Mortality, however, is accepted as a fact of life. And the gospels seem to discount an ancient belief that the tragedy of death, especially premature or violent death, or the tragedy of misfortune is to be automatically associated with the personal sin of the one suffering the tragedy:

There were some present at that very time who told him (Jesus) of the Galileans whose blood Pilate had mingled with their sacrifices. And he answered them, "Do you think that these Galileans were worse sinners than all the other Galileans, because they suffered thus? I tell you, No; but unless you repent you will all likewise perish" (Luke 13:1-3 RSV).

His disciples asked him, "Rabbi, was it his sin or that of his parents that caused him to be born blind?" "Neither," answered Jesus: "It was no sin, either of this man or of his parents. Rather, it was to let God's works show forth in him" (John 9:2-3 NAB).

Such acceptance of death as of only relative importance compared to the reality of eternal life did not remove, however, the normal human anxiety over its approach. Death is the enemy, as we saw in Paul's writings (1 Cor 15:26). And a certain dreadful anxiety can be seen in Jesus' own reaction to his impending death. In the Gospel accounts, we see that Jesus begins to "be greatly distressed and troubled," (Mark 14:33) and he prays that he may be spared the ordeal which lies before him (14:36). Jesus does not want to be left alone (14:37). He implored God "with loud cries and tears" (Heb 5:7).

Jesus teaches that death, which is aligned with evil, ultimately has no place in the kingdom which his life and teachings inaugurate:

And he called to him his twelve disciples and gave them authority over unclean spirits, to cast them out, and to heal every disease and infirmity. . . . These twelve Jesus sent out, charging them, "Heal the sick, raise the dead, cleanse lepers, cast out demons" (Matt 10:1, 5, 8 RSV).

The gospels' reference to death seems to be the straightforward reference to biological death. Unlike Paul, for whom death had a wide metaphorical usage, Jesus in the gospels hardly ever uses death as a metaphor. A notable exception is Matthew 8:22: "Follow me, and leave the dead to bury their own dead" (RSV).

John

The Gospel of John is considered the last of the New Testament gospels to have been written. It has a distinct emphasis on the present transformation of life because Jesus was raised up (both on the cross and in the resurrection), therefore winning salvation for all and fulfilling the Father's plan from the dawn of time. Actually, for John, the quality of one's existence here and now is stressed rather than concentration upon a resurrection at some unknown time beyond biological death. Eternal life begins now for those in Jesus who is the light of life already dispelling the darkness:

> Through him was life, and this life was the light of the human race; the light shines in the darkness, and the darkness has not overcome it (John 1:4 RNAB).

> Whoever believes in the Son has eternal life, but whoever disobeys the Son will not see life (3:36 RNAB).

> Whoever hears my word and believes in the one who sent me, has eternal life and will not come to condemnation, but has passed from death to life (5:24 RNAB).

With eternal life effectively beginning here and now for those in the light—in Jesus—then one can imagine how biological death is not a fundamental problem and is seldom mentioned in John. Death is actually a part of existence which followers of Jesus can transcend. They are no longer part of a death-oriented existence even though they biologically expire. Therefore, one can understand Jesus' paradoxical words to Martha: "I am the resurrection and the life; whoever believes in me, even if he dies, will live, and everyone who lives and believes in me will never die" (11:25-26 RNAB).

While the anxiety and fearfulness of Jesus' death is depicted in the Synoptic Gospels of Matthew, Mark, and Luke, Jesus' death, for John, is self-consciously seen as a deliberate and positive act:

> For this reason the Father loves me, because I lay down my life. . . . No one takes it from me, but I lay it down of my own accord. I have power to lay it down, and I have power to take it up again (10:17-18 NAB).

Likewise, we can see the contrast to Paul's emphasis on the resurrection of Jesus as the destruction of the powers of sin and death. John places equal stress on Jesus' death both as the decisive act which releases the grace of salvation and as a constructive power for his followers. Thus Jesus' saying about being raised up refers both to being raised up on the beam of the cross and to rising up in the resurrection. So Jesus can speak of the time of death as the glory awaited:

> The hour has come for the Son of man to be glorified. . . . Unless a grain of wheat falls into the earth and dies, it remains alone; but if it dies, it bears much fruit (12:23-24 NAB).

The crossing over from a mortality-bound existence to eternal life is a theme continued in the Johannine letters. The new existence possible is not only a new interior life but a life that has power to transform others. This is the dynamism of the new Christian existence:

> We know that we have passed from death to life because we love our brothers. Whoever does not love remains in death. . . . The way we came to know love was that he laid down his life for us; so we ought to lay down our lives for our brothers (1 John 3:14-16 RNAB).

In the Book of Revelation (or Apocalypse) there is a more deliberate focus on the end-time realities of death, judgment, and the vindicated life of the resurrected. This Book was written during a persecution of the early Christians late in the first century. It is encouragement Scripture enabling the saints (early Christians) of the Church to persevere. Its major thesis is that those who are suffering—or have suffered—martyrdom will be vindicated through a resurrection of the dead to enjoy a special time with Christ and will behold the final destruction of death, Satan, and all the enemies of the Church:

> He will dwell with them, and they shall be his people, and God himself will be with them; he will wipe away every tear from their eyes, and death shall be no more, neither shall there be mourning nor crying nor pain any more, for the former things have passed away (21:3-4 NAB).

Death is seen as an evil instituted by the activity of the devil, whose activity is also responsible for sickness and misfortune (9:1-11). But Christ has received the heavenly kingship, and in time that kingship will be felt throughout the world until at last his victory will extend even to the underworld where the power of Satan, Death, and Hades will be destroyed:

> And the devil who had deceived them was thrown into the lake of fire and brimstone (20:10 RSV).

> Then Death and Hades were thrown into the lake of fire. This is the second death (20:14 RSV).

The Book of Revelation is filled with often confusing imagery. However, a thorough understanding of the Old Testament, especially toward the end, as well as Jewish apocalyptic literature just before and during Christ's time, can give the reader the best clue for handling the symbolic connotations of the various symbols and numbers employed. Too often, this book has been used as if it were a padlock awaiting the discovery of the right combination for the exact date of the end of the world. Too often, followers of self-proclaimed "discoverers" of the combination have been disillusioned when the world did not end as predicted. And too often, many therefore became disillusioned with the Christian message of hope found in the Book of Revelation. How quickly the words of Jesus are forgotten concerning our inability to know when the end of the world will come:

> "As to the exact day or hour, no one knows it, neither the angels in heaven nor even the Son, but only the Father. Be constantly on the watch! Stay awake! You do not know when the appointed time will come" (Mark 13:32-33 NAB).

The New Testament, in union with Old Testament teaching, continues to teach the definitiveness of death in the biological sense. No tradition can be called forth from within Scriptures to show that humans undergo more than the one death; that is, there are no reincarnations. In fact, in the Letter to the Hebrews, such a notion is deliberately dispelled. "Just as it is appointed that men die once, and after death be judged . . . " (Heb 9:27 NAB).

The realism of the Bible is that we will not find a way to escape reality, especially that of death, but to put reality into a new context which will make all the difference. Death becomes a relative rather than an ultimate reality compared to eternal life, even though it can still be seen as an enemy humans must face until the end of time. In the meantime, death can serve the Christian believer as a challenge to more fully live this life. With a certain relativization of death—with the possibility of eternal life beginning now for the follower of Jesus—more life is possible. Life should be seen now as less bound by any paralyzing anxiety which would prevent freedom of action for the glory of God and for a full life. Yet death stands before the human person as a moment of judgment for those who would use their freedom to turn away from the glory of God.

Chapter Seven
Eternal Possibilities

By the time one comes to the end of the New Testament writings, certain realities are accepted as part and parcel of revelation about the afterlife. After death, the individual has a sense of supreme consciousness. This is the assumption in the story Jesus tells of the beggar Lazarus and the rich man (often called Dives in tradition):

> Eventually the beggar died. He was carried by angels to the bosom of Abraham. The rich man likewise died and was buried. From the abode of the dead where he was in torment, he raised his eyes and saw Abraham afar off, and Lazarus resting in his bosom. He called out, "Father Abraham, have pity on me. Send Lazarus to dip the tip of his finger in water to refresh my tongue, for I am tortured in these flames." "My child," replied Abraham, "remember that you were well off in your lifetime, while Lazarus was in misery. Now he has found consolation here, but you have found torment. And that is not all. Between you and us there is fixed a great abyss, so that those who might wish to cross from here to you cannot do so, nor can anyone cross from your side to us." "Father, I ask you, then," the rich man said, "send him to my father's house where I have five brothers. Let him be a warning to them so that they may not end in this place of torment." Abraham answered, "They have Moses and the prophets. Let them hear them" (Luke 16:22-29 NAB).

Much that is implied in this parable told by Jesus seems to be part of the mental furniture of the time. Some of these understandings were that: (a) there was an abode of the dead, (b) great figures such as Father Abraham have a role of intercession in the afterlife, (c) and consciousness in the afterlife may well extend two ways, into the eternal abodes of the afterlife as well as to realities on earth. (Cf. also 1 Cor 13:12, "My knowledge is imperfect now; then I shall know even as I am known.")

The New Testament has many strands of tradition supporting the belief that there is an abode for the dead after death. Somehow, Jesus himself visited that abode, preached there, and set free a number of the inhabitants. Paul repeats Psalm 68 and interprets it in the context of Christ:

> Thus you find Scripture saying: "When he ascended on high, he took a host of captives and gave gifts to men." "He ascended"— what does this mean but that he had first descended into the lower regions of the earth? He who descended is the very one who ascended high above the heavens. . . . " (Eph 4:8-10 NAB).

Peter writes of Christ going to the dead:

> He was put to death insofar as fleshly existence goes, but was given life in the realm of the spirit. It was in the spirit also that he went to preach to the spirits in prison (1 Pet 3:18-19 NAB).

And immediately he continues, "The reason the gospel was preached even to the dead was that, although condemned in the flesh in the eyes of men, they might live in the spirit in the eyes of God."

In Matthew, Jesus talked of his death and a time in the underworld: "So will the Son of Man spend three days and three nights in the bowels of the earth" (12:40 NAB). And in another place, Jesus made reference to the place of the dead: "As for you, Capernaum, 'Are you to be exalted to the skies? You shall go down to the realm of death!' " (Matt 11:23 NAB).

In line with the tomb being a metaphor for the dwelling of the dead, Matthew in one place speaks of the dead coming forth from such a place after the death of Jesus:

> Many bodies of saints who had fallen asleep were raised. After Jesus' resurrection they came forth from their tombs and entered the holy city and appeared to many (Matt 27:52-53 NAB).

Paul writes to the Thessalonians in his First Letter: "God will bring forth those also who have fallen asleep believing in Him" (4:13-14 NAB). Finally, Paul quotes Moses and interlaces his addition to affirm Christ's power over life and death:

> "Do not say in your heart, 'Who shall go up into heaven?' (that is, to bring Christ down), or 'Who shall go down into the abyss?' (that is, to bring Christ up from the dead)" (Rom 10:6-7 NAB).

The Book of Revelation, as we have noted, pictures this abode of the dead as a place for the just, also, who are symbolically placed under the heavenly altar to wait a little while longer before receiving their final reward (cf. Rev 6:9-11). This reference and all of the preceding references concerning the abode of the dead have exegetical problems for the modern reader (i.e., problems ascertaining the words' exact meaning in the text and their meaning, in context, at the time of writing). However, these and other passages show the strong prevalent belief that there is a situation or several situations for the dead before the end-time judgment and the final resurrection of the dead. We have touched on this briefly earlier. Various Christian faith traditions have concluded differently using this same textual data. Leaving behind this data for now, we push on to the dominant abodes of the afterlife, those situations of eternal reward and eternal punishment.

Ultimately, the afterlife becomes a matter of eternal reward or punishment. Such is the end result of the last-judgment scene Jesus portrays in Matthew 25:

> When the Son of Man comes in his glory, escorted by all the angels of heaven, he will sit upon his royal throne, and all the nations will be assembled before him. Then he will separate them into two groups. . . . The king will say to those on his right: "Come. You have my Father's blessing! Inherit the kingdom prepared for you from the creation of the world. For I was hungry and you gave me food, I was thirsty and you gave me drink." Then he will say to those on his left: "Out of my sight, you condemned, into that everlasting fire prepared for the devil and his angels! I was hungry and

you gave me no food, I was thirsty and you did not give me to drink." These will go off to eternal punishment and the just to eternal life (vv 31-46 NAB).

Earlier in the gospel, Matthew has Jesus telling his followers what to expect along these lines: "The Son of Man will come with his Father's glory accompanied by his angels. When he does, he will repay each man according to his conduct" (16:27 NAB).

It seems, though there is the reality of a final judgment, that the destiny of reward or punishment is pretty much determined at the point of death. Paul tells us that we receive our recompense "according to our life in the body" (2 Cor 5:10). While in the body, followers of Jesus must make choices and set their lives on the right course. When asked by his disciples if many or few would be saved, Jesus answered more with a challenge than a definitive answer: "Enter through the narrow gate. The gate that leads to damnation is wide, the road is clear, and many choose to travel it" (Matt 7:13 NAB).

The metaphor for eternal punishment spoken of in the New Testament tends to be that of eternal fire. We have seen that Hades, often translated as Hell, is to be more properly understood as the abode of the dead. It is not a pleasant place and within it could be found the reality of punishment or the eternal fires, as shown in the parable of Lazarus and Dives.

Apart from the usage of the metaphor of unquenchable fires, the image of Gehenna was several times employed by Jesus. This image was useful, for it probably referred to the burning dump in the valley of Gehenna immediately south of Jerusalem. In Mark, chapter 9, Jesus uses the image and provides a slight explanation: "Better for you to enter the kingdom of God with one eye than to be thrown with both eyes into Gehenna, where 'the worm dies not and the fire is never extinguished.' " Another one of several statements using Gehenna as an image is Matthew 5:22: "And if anyone holds his brother in contempt he risks the fires of Gehenna" (NAB).

The controlling imagery for eternal punishment, however, is still fire.

> His winnowing fan is in his hand. He will clear the threshing floor and gather his grain into the barn, but the chaff he will burn in unquenchable fire (Matt 3:12 NAB).

> Better to enter life maimed or crippled than be thrown with two hands or two feet into endless fire (Matt 18:8 NAB).

Or take the expanded imagery of Matthew 13:49 as an example:

> That is how it will be at the end of the world. Angels will go out and separate the wicked from the just and hurl the wicked into the fiery furnace where they will wail and grind their teeth (NAB).

And such is the imagery in the late writing of Jude (v. 7): "They are set before us to dissuade us, as they undergo a punishment of eternal fire." Such descriptions continue the imagery found in one of the Old Testament writings, Sirach 21:9: "A band of criminals is like a bundle of tow; they will end in a flaming fire."

Though such imagery is present in the New Testament in an attempt to describe some form of the mystery present in the reality of eternal punishment for those who remained opposed to God, the intent of the New Testament writings is to give hope; no one is to despair:

> God has not destined us for wrath but for acquiring salvation through our Lord Jesus Christ. He died for us, that all of us, whether awake or asleep, together might live with him (1 Thess 5:9-10 NAB).

John writes one of the great hope-filled passages of the New Testament:

> In my Father's house there are many dwelling places; otherwise, how could I have told you that I was going to prepare a place for you? I am indeed going to prepare a place for you, and then I shall come back to take you with me, that where I am you also may be (14:2-3 NAB).

Readers of the New Testament will find much material in order to dream dreams and grow ever more excited about the possibilities of the other and greatest final destiny, heaven. Ever since the revelation in Genesis (1 and 5) that humans were created in the divine image of God, it seemed natural for believers and followers of the tradition of the Bible to sense that there must be an awesome destiny in store for the afterlife.

The central motif of the New Testament is the resurrection of Jesus and our own future resurrection in the resurrection of the dead. Paul notes, "If Christ has not been raised, our preaching is void of content and your faith is empty, too" (1 Cor 15:14 NAB). In New Testament thought and throughout Christian history, the belief is held that the resurrection will perpetuate the individual, both body and soul. This will be the person's immortal, eternal identity. However, the individual will rise vastly changed in a new kind of spiritual body not subject to decay as the biological or material body had been.

It is in 1 Corinthians 15 that we have Paul presenting a lengthy treatise on the subject of the resurrection for which Christians hope. It is given as a revelation to Paul and to the Christian community, probably to answer a number of questions Christians had in making this transition in their tradition, at least the transition from an earlier tradition which included a belief in a kind of resurrection in which bodies for an earthly dwelling would be given in the Kingdom of God.

The stories of Jesus' raising the little girl in Mark 5, or returning Lazarus to life in John 11, were marvels believers could appreciate. But as Paul explained, the final resurrection is a qualitatively different reality of the body given back to the individual. It is a spiritual body, a glorified body, which we will be given in the resurrection of the dead.

> Perhaps someone will say, "How are the dead to be raised up? What kind of body will they have?" A nonsensical question! The seed you

sow does not germinate unless it dies. . . . God gives body to it as he pleases. Not all bodily nature is the same. Men have one kind of body, animals another. Birds are of their kind, fish are of theirs. There are heavenly bodies and there are earthly bodies. . . . So it is with the resurrection of the dead. What is sown in the earth is subject to decay, what rises is incorruptible. What is sown is ignoble, what rises is glorious. Weakness is sown, strength rises up. A natural body is put down and a spiritual body comes up. If there is a natural body, be sure there is also a spiritual body. . . . Just as we resemble the man from earth, so shall we bear the likeness of the man from heaven. . . . The trumpet will sound and the dead will be raised incorruptible, and we shall be changed. This corruptible body must be clothed with incorruptibility, this mortal body with immortality. When the corruptible frame takes on incorruptibility and the mortal immortality, then will the saying of Scripture be fulfilled: "Death is swallowed up in victory" (1 Cor 15:35-54 NAB).

From this treatise, the Christian tradition in several historical councils has identified qualities of the resurrected-body person. One quality is impassibility or immunity from death and pain. Another is subtility or freedom from restraint by matter. Others are agility or obedience to one's soul (spirit) with relation to movement and space, and clarity, which is refulgent beauty of the soul manifested in the body. In any event, in regard to this anticipated reality, Paul's treatise to the Corinthians is consistent with his letter to the Philippians:

He will give a new form to this lowly body of ours and remake it according to the pattern of his glorified body, by his power to subject everything to himself (3:21 NAB).

This is about as analytical as the New Testament writings get concerning a specific afterlife reality. There is a self- consciousness among the writers that they are dealing in rich imagery yet with mysterious realities, and such mystery demands a certain reserve about rational analysis. Paul did write a line much earlier in his letter to the Corinthians that inspires great hope while leveling a proper caution:

What eye has not seen, and ear has not heard, and what has not entered the human heart, what God has prepared for those who love him—this God has revealed to us through the Spirit (1 Cor 2:9 RNAB).

Another favorite imagery through the ages is one spoken by Jesus to the repentant and believing criminal crucified with him, the imagery of paradise: "He then said, 'Jesus, remember me when you enter upon your reign.' And Jesus replied, 'I assure you; this day you will be with me in paradise' " (Luke 23:42-43 NAB). Concerning this passage that includes the word "paradise", William Barclay writes:

> The very sound of the word is lovely. It may be that we do not attach any very definite meaning to it but when we study history, we come upon some of the most adventurous thinking the world has ever known.[16]

In his analysis, Barclay states that the word "paradise" is of Persian origin and was introduced into the Greek language. Originally, it meant a pleasure garden, even several gardens, where a king, for instance, could walk. They were gardens he owned. In the Greek version of the Old Testament, the Septuagint, paradise has two uses—it is regularly used for the Garden of Eden (Gen 2, 3); secondly, it is used of any stately garden (Isa 1:30; Jer 29:5; Qoh 2:5).

Part of the ancient imagery of the garden is the conception of the tree of life. This is part of the story of the garden of Eden where in its midst was the tree of life (cf. Gen 2:9). Later in Jewish thought, this tree came to be a symbol for that which gave humans life. And so Wisdom is pictured as a tree of life to those who lay hold of her (Prov 3:18). The fruit of the righteous is a tree of life as is hope fulfilled (Prov 11:30, 13:12).

The garden-of-paradise imagery would not be complete without realizing that Adam (the human) was barred from the garden when he had eaten of another tree's fruit which God had forbidden to the humans. In this expulsion, the

---

[16]William Barclay, *The Revelation of John,* vol. 1 of the "Daily Bible Series" (Philadelphia: Westminster, 1976) 69. Barclay, 69–71, will be used for the analysis of this word and imagery of paradise.

tree of life was lost to them forever. But it was a Jewish conception that, when the Messiah came and the new age dawned, the tree of life would be in the midst of the human race and those who had been faithful would eat of it. So states Sirach 19:19: "They that do the things that please you (God), shall receive the fruit of the tree of immortality."* The rabbis had a picture of the tree of life in paradise; it had five hundred thousand fragrant perfumes and its fruit had as many pleasant tastes, every one of them different. So, to have access to the tree of life in the garden of paradise and to eat of its fruit was to have all the joys God could provide.

The great early Christian thinkers (e.g., Tertullian, Philo, Origen) did not identify paradise automatically with heaven. Barclay notes:

> Paradise was the intermediate stage, where the souls of the righteous were fitted to enter the presence of God. There is something very lovely here. Who has not felt that the leap from earth to heaven is too great for one step and that there is need of a gradual entering into the presence of God?[17]

However, after centuries of usage, paradise did not retain this original meaning in most peoples' beliefs or theologies. It gradually came to be equivalent to heaven.

The Book of Revelation has popularized the imagery of heaven as a kind of glorious royal city; so is the new holy city of Jerusalem pictured in chapter 21. It is a four-sided, square city with great walls and splendid gates incorporating the most precious stones and metals known to humankind, and full of the most radiant light from the glory of God. The streets are like gold. It has plenty of water and trees of life. If John were a person used to the desert, one can imagine then how great this imagery would have been to him. We

---

*A verse found as an addition in Sirach, of Gr. II (RSVm). The figure of the "tree of immortality" is derived ultimately from Genesis 2:9; 3:22-24, and is applied to the spiritual life in Proverbs (3:18; 11:30; 13:12; 15:4). It is found in descriptions of the next world in apocryphal literature (1 Enoch, 2 Enoch, Test. Levi 18:11, 4 Esdras), and signifies the happiness of heaven in Revelation 22:2, 14, 19.

[17]*Idem*, Barclay, 71.

remember that this is imagery which is meant to entice the reader. This John or the John who wrote the Gospel proclaimed that heaven is always a mystery: "No one has gone up to heaven except the One who came down from there—the Son of Man (who is in heaven)" (3:13).

The imagery of the Book of Revelation about the realities of heaven attempt to appeal to the senses with the most pleasant earthly realities known, things holy yet pleasing to sight, to hearing, to smelling. Such imagery is meant to increase the hearer's or the reader's longing. The smell of heaven is aroused by the imagery of incense:

> Another angel came in holding a censer of gold. He took his place at the altar of incense and was given large amounts of incense to deposit on the altar of gold in front of the throne, together with the prayers of all God's holy ones. From the angel's hand the smoke of the incense went up before God, and with it the prayers of God's people (8:3-4 NAB).

There was also the smell of aromatic spices and the sounds of music. The imagery of the harp evoked one of the most pleasant sounds known at the time of the writing of this book. Thus the ear could long for the beauty of the sounds of heaven: "Along with their harps, the elders were holding vessels of gold filled with aromatic spices, which were the prayers of God's holy people" (5:8 NAB). There were loud noises in heaven, to be sure, heard by the visionary, but they were tempered by the melodious sound of the harpists and a heavenly choir:

> I heard a sound from heaven which resembled the roaring of the deep, or loud peals of thunder; the sound I heard was like the melody of harpists playing on their harps. They were singing a new hymn before the throne, in the presence of the four living creatures and the elders. This hymn no one could learn except the hundred and forty-four thousand who had been ransomed from the world (14:2-3 NAB).

Gold was the color as well as the metal chosen as most pleasing to the sight. It did not rust or change its appearance through the ages, thus reflecting eternity. It has always been a precious commodity, but the color was sometimes thought to reflect the sun and its brightness. The Book of Revelation is filled with this color. Many of the figures of the visions wore crowns of gold. The altar was golden as were the vessels of worship and much of the new heavenly city of Jerusalem. All this is meant to captivate the eye and transfix the beholding person in awe.

Another image used in Matthew's Gospel is the kingdom of Heaven. Many scholars think that this expression, found only in Matthew's Gospel, is the same as the expression "kingdom of God" used in Mark and Luke's Gospels. Matthew may have substituted the word "heaven" for "God" because many early Christians, especially converts from Judaism, would have wanted to continue the Jewish belief that God's name was too holy to pronounce or write. It is not known for sure which expression Jesus may have used.[18] However, the most common expression in the gospels is "kingdom of God," which will be the expression we use in this summary. The possibility that Matthew may have substituted a word shows the close association these two words and their corresponding realities had.

The kingdom of God is a New Testament image. It refers to eternal realities, but for the believer, it includes this earthly life. It probably can be best defined as the sovereignty, reign, or rule of God in Jesus Christ: "And his reign will be without end" (Luke 1:33). Thus the reality of the kingdom began with the coming of Jesus in his humanity.

There are the dual qualities of "already" and "not yet" about the kingdom of God. In Mark, Jesus came preaching the gospel of the kingdom announcing that the kingdom was at hand (cf. Mark 1:14-15): "Say to them, 'The reign of God is at hand' " (Luke 10:9 NAB). The basic message of Jesus

---

[18]*Harper's Bible Dictionary,* Paul Achtemeier, ed. (San Francisco: Harper & Row, 1985) 528. Cf. C. H. Dodd, *The Parables of the Kingdom,* rev. ed. (New York: Scribner, 1961).

and his disciples was that the kingdom of God had come near. Jesus taught his followers in the Lord's Prayer to pray for its coming (Matt 6:10; Luke 11:2).

Those who live in accordance with God's will can hope to enter the kingdom (Matt 5:3-10, 7:21-23). If the reader takes seriously John's writing, "Whoever believes in the Son has life eternal," (3:36) then that person can observe how the kingdom is already present in some way. It is present in the person of Jesus, the living Messiah, and in the final coming of the kingdom, as well as in the life and faith of those who respond by repenting and changing their lives when they come to believe in Jesus as the Messiah, the Son of the living God. There are various parables that help with this interpretation: cf. Mark 4:30f; Matthew 13:33; Luke 13:20f; Matthew 12:28; Luke 11:20; Luke 17:20f.

The imagery of the kingdom of God is another happy way for the New Testament to fill readers with an anticipation of heaven. For most of New Testament writing, the kingdom of God is about inheriting it, entering it, or having citizenship in it. Like the Jesus of John's Gospel who promised believers eternal life in the heavenly mansions (John 14:1-3), Paul looked for the new life of the transformed in a heavenly citizenship (Phil 3:20-21). The Book of Revelation looked for the establishment of God's kingdom both in heaven and on earth (11:15, 12:10), and speaks of it as a new heaven and a new earth (21:1). Finally, the New Jerusalem would come down from heaven (Rev 21:2, 10) and God and the Lamb would "reign for ever and ever" (22:5).

The judgment scene of Matthew 25 combines the image of the kingdom with blessed happiness for those who enter heaven: "Come. You have my Father's blessing! Inherit the kingdom prepared for you from the creation of the world" (25:34 NAB).

In rich imagery, combining many of the traditions of the old covenant with the new, the author of the Book of Hebrews speaks of the followers of Jesus, how close they are to their awesome reward:

> You have drawn near to Mt. Zion and the city of the living God, the heavenly Jerusalem, to myriads of angels in festal gathering, to the assembly of the firstborn enrolled in heaven, to God the judge of all, to the spirits of just men made perfect, to Jesus, the mediator of the new covenant (12:22-24 NAB).

Such a festal gathering of folk shows the absence of aloneness or loneliness in the reality of heaven.

Whatever the imagery employed, New Testament writers add that what awaits is wonderfully beyond present limited human imagination: "What eye has not seen, and ear has not heard, and what has not entered the human heart, what God has prepared for those who love him" (1 Cor 2:9 RNAB). Or rejoice with John, "We are God's children now. What we shall later be has not yet come to light. We know that when it comes to light we shall be like him, for we shall see him as he is" (1 John 3:2 NAB).

In talking of the greatest reality of love, Paul notes,

> Now we see indistinctly, as in a mirror; then we shall see face to face. My knowledge is imperfect now; then I shall know even as I am known. There are in the end three things that last: faith, hope, and love, and the greatest of these is love (1 Cor 13:12-13 NAB).

The lasting reality of love is the most heavenly reality, after death, that we can dream. It is the divine reality that the revelation in Jesus brought. As 2 Timothy 1:10 attests, it was only when Jesus brought "life and immortality to light through the gospel" that it became clearer what the destiny of the soul is after death.

After reviewing the profound imagery of heavenly happiness held out in the New Testament writings, we hope that the reader will more enthusiastically desire to contemplate the Scriptures and what they have to say on death and destiny. Christians, with their transformed view of reality, of life, death, and the afterlife, can say with St. Paul, "Oh death, where is your victory? O death, where is your sting?" (1 Cor 15:55 NAB).

Additional Reading

Bailey Sr., Lloyd R. *Biblical Perspectives on Death*. Philadelphia: Fortress Press, 1979.

Berger, Badham, et al., eds. *Perspectives on Death and Dying: Cross-cultural and Multi-disciplinary Views*. Philadelphia: Charles, 1989.

Nevins, Albert J. *Life after Death*. Huntington: Our Sunday Visitor, 1983.

Rogerson, J. W. *Anthropology and the Old Testament*. Oxford, 1978.

Wolff, H. W. *Anthropologie des Alten Testament*. Munich: 1973. (Also available in English)

Leon-Dufour, Xavier. *Life and Death in the New Testament*. Trans. by T. Prendergast. San Francisco: Harper & Row, 1979.